Modern Writers

Alan Bold

**George
Mackay Brown**

G. MACKAY BROWN

Oliver & Boyd
Edinburgh

Oliver & Boyd

Croythorn House
23 Ravelston Terrace
Edinburgh EH4 3TJ
A Division of Longman Group Ltd.

ISBN 0 05 003089 2 Cased
     0 05 003090 6 Paperback

Printed by Sing Cheong Printing Co. Ltd.
Bound by Ching Yick Printing & Book Binding Co.

Contents

Acknowledgements

First of all I would like to thank George Mackay Brown for his co-operation; his detailed answers to questions of mine provided valuable insights into his creative approach. Some of these answers have been included in the text. I have known George personally for a decade and on my two most recent visits to Orkney spent several pleasant evenings with him, in Stromness, over the excellent ale. (With Orkney itself I have had a protracted love-affair since the age of thirteen when I spent an unforgettable summer on Dounby farm.) Thanks are also due to George's publisher, Mrs Norah Smallwood of The Hogarth Press, for assistance with practical matters. I am also grateful to my friend David Morrison of Wick—Divisional Librarian with the Highland Region—for supplying me with books which would otherwise have been difficult to obtain. For permission to quote copyright material acknowledgements are due to The Hogarth Press for quotations from *Magnus, Hawkfall, The Sun's Net, The Two Fiddlers, Fishermen with Ploughs, Loaves and Fishes, The Year of the Whale, Poems New and Selected, Winterfold, A Spell for Green Corn*; The Hogarth Press and Harcourt Brace Jovanovich, Inc. for quotations from *Greenvoe, A Calendar of Love*, and *A Time to Keep*; to Victor Gollancz Ltd. for quotations from *An Orkney Tapestry* and to the Editor of *Chapman* for quotations from that journal.

1   Orkneyman

Since the literary revolution initiated by the 'men of 1914'—Joyce, Pound, Eliot, Wyndham Lewis—the label 'international' has been pinned to every writer whose formal method is fragmentary and whose abiding theme is the *ennui* of exile. It is a heavy label and those who have had to bear it show signs of having stooped too long over influential books and spurious critical theories. Modernism has become a library phenomenon with only a tenuous hold on the facts of life. When critical orthodoxy has admitted an alternative to modernism it has recognised another extreme: documentary realism where significance is synonymous with a no-nonsense account of the surface of life.

It is impossible to place George Mackay Brown into either of these literary camps. His work, not being determined by the dictates of a critical theory, has neither the gimmickry of modernism nor the quasi-photographic fidelity of documentary realism. In other words he is something of a law unto himself: a man activated by a wide artistic vision. He does not deal with squalid city life but reveals a great island landscape that takes in the ruined crofts at Rackwick, the standing stones of Stenness and Brodgar, the Maes Howe burial chamber, the great red sandstone cathedral in Kirkwall. His personal pantheon includes real saints like Magnus and Rognvald as well as imaginary sinners like the timeless tinkers who populate many of his stories and poems. He is a deeply religious man, a convert to Catholicism, who has a contempt for the contemporary faith in Progress. He writes of crofters and fishermen and monks and Vikings and all his work is informed with legend and myth and image and symbol. He is very much his own man.

George Mackay Brown was born on 17 October 1921 in Stromness, the little seaport on the south-west corner of the Orkney mainland that has remained the centre of his creative universe. He has left his parish and his island only occasionally yet those conveniently dismissive epithets 'parochial' and 'insular' could never be applied to Brown's writing which abounds in universal implications. It is worth remembering that when Robert Burns published the Kilmarnock edition of his *Poems, Chiefly in the Scottish Dialect* in 1786 he had never set foot outside his native Ayrshire; in a similar way Brown has found everything he needs, artistically, in Orkney and everything he writes is rooted in the incredibly rich prehistory, recorded past and modern life of the islands.

Stromness, with its single serpentine street of flagstones, its tiny closes, its "pipe-spitting pierhead" (as Brown calls it in his poem 'Hamnavoe') has less than two thousand inhabitants but, as readers of Brown will know, has had more than its fair share of characters. In his poems and stories Brown prefers the Norse name Hamnavoe (meaning haven-bay) for the town where his father, John Brown, was born in 1875. A tailor to trade, John Brown found his livelihood threatened by the growing demand for ready-made clothes so he became a postman and kept his tailoring as a sideline. In 1910 John Brown married the nineteen-year-old Mhairi Sheena Mackay, a native Gaelic speaker and one of nine children of a crofter-fisherman in Strathy, Sutherland. She had come to Stromness to work in a hotel owned by John Mackay, a relative. John and Mhairi Brown produced six children, a girl and five boys (one of whom died in infancy). George Mackay Brown was the youngest of the family.

Brown has fond memories of his parents. His father he remembers as a great egalitarian; a Labour man with a passion for hymns and music-hall ballads; a complex moody man who liked to recall that he had twice seen the Salvation Army's William Booth addressing a mass rally in Glasgow. When his father became ill with arthritis George would go to Stromness library to fetch books for him (especially books about economic hardship). He died early in World War Two:

> I think the notion that he had four sons that could be taken for military service hurt him a lot. After the fall of France in May 1940, he said to my mother, 'Thank God, none of the boys will have to go to France now. . . .' He died suddenly of coronary thrombosis, a few weeks later.*

*All unspecified quotations are taken from correspondence with George Mackay Brown.

Mhairi Brown survived her husband by twenty-seven years:

> She had the sweetest nature of any person I have known; everybody liked and trusted her. Her health was not particularly good (asthma, mainly) and she had worries about money, &c., but cheerfulness kept breaking through the crust. She always sang as she went about her housework: a kind of low happy monotone.

As there was nothing particularly literary about the Brown household there was simply no reason for his parents to encourage George to write. No one else in the family showed a talent that way. The poet's three brothers became bartender, banker and teacher and his sister also became a teacher. It was when he went to school, Stromness Academy, that George Mackay Brown gradually realised that he had a gift for writing:

> I first began to think I might have some ability as a writer when at the age of seven or eight we had to write compositions for our teacher . . . I found to my astonishment that I always wrote the best composition. . . . Writing compositions [was] all that I shone at in the dark prison of school. I believe with scripture that every person has a talent of some kind, a creative gift, and he must spend the rest of his life trying to perfect it. . . . So then, I did have this gift with language. It is a gift you do not ask for nor work for. It is a grace given for no apparent merit, but once you know you have it the rest of your days are spent perfecting it as well as you know how, in order to try to understand yourself and the world you live in.*

Brown attended Stromness Academy from 1926 to 1940. With characteristic modesty he says, "I wasn't very bright, had to have two attempts at what was called the Higher Leaving Certificate before I passed". He felt no particular ambition to do anything that would lead to a respectable life of "Getting and spending" (a phrase from Wordsworth's sonnet 'The world is too much with us' that he is

*Chapman, vol. iv., no. 4, summer 1976, p. 21.

extremely fond of quoting). In the event illness intervened. A year after leaving school he was admitted to the sanatorium at Kirkwall suffering from tuberculosis. That more or less imposed a period of introspection on him and he "thereafter wasn't allowed to work, except at light things like local reporting, for years". He spent most of his time reading, and writing the occasional poem. Living on National Assistance was a tiresome strain for Brown and he was very interested indeed when in the spring of 1951 Alex Doloughan, Director of Further Education for Orkney, asked him if he would like to go to Newbattle Abbey, a residential adult education college in Dalkeith, near Edinburgh.

The college had been established in 1936 but had closed down with the outbreak of war. In 1950 it reopened with Edwin Muir as Warden. George Mackay Brown had read Muir's *The Story and the Fable* (1940) in which the raw material of Orkney was transmuted into the stuff of myth and legend. It was one of the books that most influenced his own approach to life and literature. Now Muir and his wife Willa were spending their summer holidays of 1951 in Orkney. Brown was introduced to the Muirs, by Alex Doloughan, and had tea with them in Stromness Hotel. The outcome was that in October 1951 George Mackay Brown went to Newbattle for "probably the happiest year of my life".

Muir was, by all accounts, a wonderfully sympathetic teacher and man and he was particularly anxious to encourage creative work, especially that of his fellow Orkneyman, George Mackay Brown, whose poems he deeply admired. Muir recommended one of Brown's poems, 'The Exile', to the *New Statesman* and it was duly published on 5 April 1952: "The other students were quite impressed", Brown remembers, "I was more surprised than anything". A year after this national poetic debut Brown was back in the Kirkwall sanatorium with another attack of TB and after fifteen months treatment he came out "into the same workless situation as before. . . . I really couldn't face more drift and meaninglessness". However a book of Brown's poems, *The Storm*, was published by The Orkney Press in 1954 and Muir contributed a glowing introduction: "I am a great admirer of George Brown's poetry. . . . He has the gift of imagination and the gift of words: the poet's endowment".

Although Muir had left Newbattle in the summer of 1955 to become Charles Eliot Norton Professor at Harvard, Brown returned for a second spell at Newbattle in summer 1956 to prepare himself for entry to an English course at Edinburgh university the same year. By this time Muir was really urging Brown into print, offering him encouragement and practical help. Writing from his hotel in Cambridge, Mass., on 9 April 1956 Muir told Brown:

> I admire these poems of yours more and more the more I read them: you have a feeling for words which I sincerely envy! . . . The genius is there, my dear George, and I wish you all that it offers you. I still think you should prepare a volume of your best poems up to now.*

This was a magnanimous gesture on the part of a man whose *Collected Poems: 1921–51* (1952) had established him as one of the finest living English poets. On 6 March 1958 Muir sent a collection of Brown's poems to Mrs Norah Smallwood of The Hogarth Press and was absolutely delighted when she accepted them for publication. "I was surprised", Brown recollects, "one day in 1958, staying in digs at Marchmont Crescent [in Edinburgh], to get a letter from Hogarth Press saying they'd like to publish a book of my poems. A typescript had been sent to them by Edwin Muir. . . . Myself, I'm quite sure I'd have done little or nothing in the way of getting them published." The book was published, as *Loaves and Fishes*, in 1959.

In 1960 Brown graduated from Edinburgh university with a second-class honours degree in English Literature. Almost immediately he had another mild attack of TB and recuperated at Tor-Na-Dee Sanatorium in Aberdeen. When he recovered his health he applied to do postgraduate work on Gerard Manley Hopkins as a result of which he was back at Edinburgh university from 1962 to 1964. The publication of *The Year of the Whale* in 1965 consolidated his reputation as a poet; while the appearance of *A Calendar of Love* in 1967 won him a new position as an eminent writer of short stories. Since his final period at Edinburgh university he has remained at Stromness (moving to a house in Mayburn Court after the death of his mother in 1967), producing his fine poetry and the stories that

*Ed. P. H. Butter, *Selected Letters of Edwin Muir*, London (The Hogarth Press) 1974, p. 184.

have made him, to my mind, one of the finest living prose stylists. Recognition has come his way slowly but surely. In 1965 he received an Arts Council grant for poetry; and in 1968 a Society of Authors' Travel Award enabled him to visit Ireland. The publication of *A Time to Keep* in 1969 brought him a Scottish Arts Council Literature prize and, for the title story, a Katherine Mansfield Menton short-story prize. In 1974 he was awarded the OBE.

George Mackay Brown is an unassuming, genuinely modest man content with a simple life. He has his friends and his books and his interest in home-made ale (something every Orkney household worth its malt takes a pride in). The international celebrity of his work has meant that in the summer he has a steady stream of admirers coming to Mayburn Court. Whatever the distractions, though, Brown makes sure he works for three hours every morning feeling it is "amazing how much can be done if you keep up a regular pace". As for his method:

> Sometimes I write very fast. I'm rapidly coming to the conclusion that my best stuff is always done quickly. In some puritanical way I used to think it a creditable thing to work hard at a poem or a story, delve into the guts to get it out. But now it seems to me I have somehow botched the things I toiled and sweated over. When I come to an impasse nowadays I put the thing away for a week or a month; generally, looked at again, the way forward is plain and obvious.

Brown's work has been shaped, above all, by the experience of living a lifetime in Orkney. It is an archipelago whose contours were formed by the Ice Age and whose history stretches back to the Stone Age. The evidence of antiquity is everywhere, in the undulations of Hoy and the spectacle of the prehistoric monoliths and megalithic tombs. It is this sense of antiquity, no doubt, that accounts for one of Brown's favourite phrases—"very ancient"—as in "very ancient rain" (*A Time to Keep*, p. 76), "very ancient wisdom" (*Hawkfall*, p. 168), "very ancient relationship" (*The Sun's Net*, p. 257), "very ancient sea sorrow" (*The Two Fiddlers*, p. 67). While expertly manipulating sequential time in his work Brown introduces a fourth dimension of timelessness wherein things happen regardless of chronology. Situations recur over centuries and the same characters walk through many generations. It is this timelessness that gives Brown's writing such intimations of the eternal: the quintessential facts of life, love and death endure the passing of the years for "time is not a conflagration; it is a slow grave sequence of grassblade, fish, apple, star, snowflake" (*Greenvoe*, p. 265).

Writing mainly of crofters and fishermen has made Brown aware of the elemental relationship these folk have with, respectively, the soil and the sea. He is exquisitely aware, too, of the four seasons that overcome the earth as it moves on its annual odyssey round the sun. One of Brown's great images concerns the circle of life, a sunwards ritual dance of seedtime, birth, harvest, death, a "potent mysterious wheel of being" (*Magnus*, p. 164). The crofter in his field, the fisherman in his boat: they are taken up in the rhythms of this great dance and its movement gives dignity to their otherwise hard lives. In conveying the rhythm of this dance Brown follows a folk tradition where "The rhythms of art were closely related to the seasonal rhythms, to a dark potent chthonic energy that raised cornstalk and rose from their roots underground" (*An Orkney Tapestry*, p. 131*).

Brown's renewal of the folk consciousness is no cerebral exercise, no erudite essay in nostalgia. He has spent a lifetime watching the corn rise and die then reappear as bread and ale; he has felt the rhythms of the waves as they smash against the Orkney coastline. The miracle of the loaves and fishes is something he perceives in the way crofters and fishermen wrench a living from the obdurate soil and the vindictive sea. His religious attitude to life derives from such personal observation and naturally a religious faith pervades everything Brown writes so that the corn always rises like a symbol of resurrection, for "I believe that [Christ] came up out of the grave the way a cornstalk soars into wind and sun from a ruined cell" (*Hawkfall*, p. 197). The plough, too, is a symbol of fertility for it digs into the past—in Orkney ploughmen sometimes turn up neolithic implements or Viking relics—and brings forth life. The plough is "like a great key to open the winter field to the sun and full bounty of harvest" (*Magnus*, p. 12). Brown's symbolism—taking the symbol to be an object that embodies an ideal—is not an arid literary device

---

*Page references for *An Orkney Tapestry* are to the paperback edition; all other page references are to hardback editions.

but something that is rooted in his profound knowledge of life in an agricultural community.

A seminal (literally) concept in Brown's work is the planting of seed as a sacred ritual. The earth is penetrated by the plough so that seed can be planted; women are penetrated by men so that human seed can be planted and the race can flourish. In *Greenvoe*, Skarf, the marxist fisherman, reconstructs the history of Hellya and imagines a Mediterranean people bringing "(very precious—guard it, watchman, with your life, for it is life and the promise of life) the jar of seed corn" (p. 29), while the poet's preface to *Fishermen with Ploughs* gives the salient fact about the Norse settlers of Rackwick: "The cargo in their hold is a jar of seed corn." As with so many of Brown's symbols this is no mere fancy but a fact on which his imagination has worked wonders; for in 1939 Dr Hans Helbaek, a Danish scientist, examined the chambered cairn of Unstan and discovered grain impressions (probably bere, a type of barley) on the neolithic pottery—evidence that the settlers of 4000 years before had indeed brought seed-corn with them.

Thus most aspects of Brown's work have both a human and a symbolic application, a temporal and a timeless dimension. Real flesh-and-blood women enliven many of Brown's poems and stories, but women become, in symbolic terms, seed-jars, vessels to receive male seed so they can perpetuate the species. To the captain in the prose finale of *Fishermen with Ploughs* "the women are nothing but walking wombs, seed jars" (p. 94), while in a poem in the first section of the same sequence, 'Gudrun', the girl remembers:

> He turned on me soon with thrustings of sun seed.
> *Thou sweet grain jar*, said Njal.

Such a basic image does not debase humanity. Instead it reminds us that we have evolved from functional beings with animal appetites into creatures capable of transcending the purely functional through the media of philosophy and art and, most central to Brown's purpose, religion. Brown likes to give a symbolic kiss of life to all things. Each substance casts its spiritual shadow. It is all part of a symbolic system where the sun is paternal, the moon moody and maternal, and the earth is the revolving stage on which human events are displayed. In this way Orkney in general, and Stromness in particular, assume a massive significance.

Some five miles from Stromness there is the chambered cairn of Maes Howe, the finest megalithic tomb in Britain. Apart from its immense archeological importance it has fired Brown's imagination in a striking way. Each midwinter, as he personally confirmed in 1972, the light of the setting sun penetrates the approach passage of Maes Howe to shine on the furthest wall of the tomb. Clearly this has sexual connotations: it is as if the sun had sown its seed in the womb-like shape of Maes Howe. The image is used in *An Orkney Tapestry*, is suggested in the title-story of *Hawkfall*, and occurs at a crucial stage of 'A Winter Tale' in *The Sun's Net*. It is a ceremonial part of Brown's fascination with birth and resurrection. Another feature of Maes Howe is that—as an archaeological investigation of 1861 showed—the walls are covered in Old Norse runic inscriptions made in the twelfth century by men who went to Jerusalem with Earl Rognvald.

Maes Howe is not, however, an isolated treasure. It lies within the Stenness-Brodgar complex along with the Ring of Brodgar, the Stenness Stones, the Ring of Bookan and Unstan Cairn (where the impressions of seed-corn were found). The twenty-seven extant stones standing in the great circle of Brodgar have provoked endless speculation as to their purpose; Brown has incorporated the phenomenon as the Temple of the Sun in *Hawkfall* while the area is used as the landscape of 'Brig-o-Dread' in *The Sun's Net*. In Orkney stones have stood through the centuries: they testify to the endurance of the past. Due to the impact of fierce sea winds Orkney is a largely treeless world, and because the Orkney people have built in stone their constructions have stood the test of time. For Brown stones have a sacred quality: his poetic ideal is the permanence of runic cuttings in stone, and the bible has Christ rising from the dead when the stone is removed. The atmosphere Brown seeks to create in his stories and poems is, to use a phrase from his sonnet 'Chapel Between Cornfield and Shore' (*Loaves and Fishes*), "A solid round of stone and ritual".

The past constantly impinges on the present in Orkney in an artistically fertile fashion. Even a simple record of Orcadian relics would reveal an archipelago visited by Iron Age broch-builders, Picts, Vikings, Scots. The triumph of Brown's writing depends on the depth of his imaginative response to such a history. He is possessed by Orkney's pageant. It is not simply the prehistoric monoliths and megalithic tombs, or the Atlantic making fantastic patterns as it eats away at the sandstone cliffs of the Orkney coastline. It is the sheer dramatic pressure of Orkney's past. For example in 1919 a shattered skull was found in a pillar of the choir of St Magnus Cathedral: this discovery of the saint's skull was a grisly confirmation of the saga account of Magnus's death. Or there is the fact that while Brown lives in a modern council house, with his television and transistor radio and his pipe and his plastic bucket of home-made ale, he still lives with the past: "I can see from the window ... the stretch of water where Gow's pirate ship anchored in 1725, and, beyond, the lovely skyline of Orphir" (*Letters from Hamanvoe*, p. 66).

This inescapable appreciation of the past has made Brown suspicious of the mechanical trappings of the present and he is an avowed enemy of progress with its tendency to obliterate tradition:

> I often think we are not really interested in the past at all. There is a new religion, Progress, in which we all devoutly believe, and it is concerned only with material things in the present and in a vague golden-handed future. It is a rootless utilitarian faith, without beauty or mystery; a kind of blind unquestioning belief that men and their material circumstances will go on improving until some kind of nirvana is reached and everyone will be rich, free, fulfilled, well-informed, masterful. . . . The notion of progress is a cancer that makes an elemental community look better, and induces a false euphoria, while it drains the life out of it remorselessly. (*An Orkney Tapestry*, p. 20 and pp. 50–1).

The pessimism that pervades much of Brown's work comes, therefore, from a fear that an addiction to progress will deprive Orcadians of their heritage and drive them into big cities (in a grotesque parody of Edwin Muir's fall from his Orkney Eden into the Glasgow Inferno). An apprehension of the death of small communities adds tension to Brown's work as he explores the possibility that the depopulation of the islands will leave behind, in terms of humanity, only the dead in the graveyards.

Against this antipathy to progress Brown sets his positive faith in the sanctity of life. As a child he had gone through the motions of religion with some distaste for the drab presbyterian services:

My parents were not deeply religious though they brought the whole family to church every Sunday. (My father could be very satirical about some ministers and elders.) There we sat and ate sweets during the long boring sermons. My father sang the hymns and psalms with gusto: he had a good light tenor voice.

In his mid-teens he began to take an interest in Catholicism:

> I was intrigued by the majesty and mystery [of Catholicism]: the long history of the church from that stark beginning, that incredibly endured through the changing centuries, always adapting itself; enriched by all that poetry and music, art and architecture, could give; and still apparently as strong as ever in our gray twentieth century.

In 1961 he became a Roman Catholic though it was no sudden conversion. He had always been interested in religious images—the ploughman lifting stones as a prelude to the resurrection of the corn—and always been fascinated by the life of Orkney's own saint, Magnus.

Basic to his religious thinking is Christ's parable of the sower and the seed:

> That image seemed to illuminate the whole of life for me. It made everything simple and marvellous. It included within itself everything from the most primitive breaking of the soil to Christ himself with his parables of agriculture and the majestic symbolism of his passion, and death, and resurrection. 'I am the bread of life.' 'This is my body that is broken for you.' That image has a universal meaning for me, especially when I can stand among ripening fields all summer. You will find it at the heart of many of my stories and poems.*

Brown's religious faith is not all affirmation, though. It has a negative side in his dislike of the Reformation and all its works. In his prologue to *The Storm* he calls Scotland "the Knox-ruined nation"; the Reformers stalk like servants of the devil in his poems and stories.

---

* *Chapman*, vol. iv., no. 4, summer 1976, p. 23.

In 'Master Halcrow, Priest' (*A Calendar of Love*) the religious images are brutally and iconoclastically destroyed by the Reformers; in *A Spell for Green Corn* the Reformation has eliminated the old faith of the island folk in the name of a rootless Progress. We are reminded of Edwin Muir's opinion that "What Knox really did was to rob Scotland of all the benefits of the Renaissance." *Brown believes that it is the business of art to recreate the miraculous atmosphere once associated with religion, to rescue the Word of God from the cold hands of ministers of the kirk:

> The Word was imprisoned between black boards, and chained and padlocked, in the pulpit of the kirk—impossible for it to get free among the ploughs and the nets, that season of famine. Therefore the lesser word, the fiddle, the poem, the rune, must work the miracle of bread. (*A Spell for Green Corn*, pp. 90–1)

Apart from the powerful influence of the bible and of Roman Catholic rituals, George Mackay Brown has been stylistically influenced by several writers: Thomas Mann, E. M. Forster, Jorge Luis Borges, Brecht, Eliot, Hopkins, Yeats, Dylan Thomas. More immediate than the impact of those writers has been the literature of Orkney. The *Orkneyinga Saga* is not, strictly speaking, an Orcadian production but a thirteenth-century work composed and compiled in Iceland. Still, it has served as a source-book of historical information for Brown as well as teaching him the merits of an unfussy narrative immediacy. Originally designed for recitation in Icelandic halls it tells the story of the Earls of Orkney from 874 to 1214 with an admirable regard for accuracy. It is a prose composition that includes eighty-three skaldic poems by eighteen skalds. The most important of these poets, from Brown's point of view, is Earl Rognvald Kolson and in *Winterfold* eight of Rognvald's poems are reworked into modern English. Brown's knowledge of the *Orkneyinga Saga*—like his poetic imitation of Rognvald—is based on the translation by A. B. Taylor published in Edinburgh (by Oliver and Boyd) in 1938.

*Edwin Muir, *John Knox—Portrait of a Calvinist*, London (Jonathan Cape) 1929, p. 309.

The work of many urban writers is personal to the point of solipsism and deracinated to the point of vacuity. Brown has cultivated an impersonal, objective, direct style—like that of the sagas or the Scottish ballads—where the narrator is conspicuous by his absence. When he writes in the first person he does so with a definite fictional persona (except in the case of the autobiographical story 'The Tarn and the Rosary' in *Hawkfall*). The saga style is uncluttered by irrelevant details and it eschews opinionated digressions. It is absolutely to the point. Brown has modelled his basic narrative technique on the simplicity of the sagas then enriched the style by the use of symbolism and the presence of euphony.

Apart from the *Orkneyinga Saga* practically nothing remains in literature of the Viking period in Orkney. From 876, when Harold I of Norway conquered Orkney, until 1471 when Scotland annexed the islands, Orkney was a Norse archipelago. Most of the placenames in Orkney have a Norse origin but the abrupt transition to the English language killed off the Norse culture. Traditional Orkney literature is confined to vernacular pieces like the 'New Year's Song' and several ballads—'The Lady Odivere' (which Brown worked into his *An Orkney Tapestry* and used as the basis for his story 'The Seal King' in *The Two Fiddlers*), 'The Grey Selchie' and 'The Great Silkie of Sule Skerry'—which tell of the transformation of seal to human, a metamorphosis incorporated by Brown in his story 'Sealskin' (*Hawkfall*).

Modern Orkney has a strong literary tradition. In the twentieth century the islands have produced three major writers in Edwin Muir, Eric Linklater and George Mackay Brown. There are also minor Orkney writers who have influenced Brown: John Firth, a Finstown joiner, celebrated the ritual of agricultural life in his *Reminiscences of an Orkney Parish* (1922); John Mooney, a Kirkwall businessman, wrote a fine biography of *Saint Magnus—Earl of Orkney* (1935); Robert Rendall, a Kirkwall draper, wrote dialect poems the best of which Brown considers to be "as good as anything that has been published in Scotland this century" (*An Orkney Tapestry*, p. 15). Undoubtedly, though, the biggest influence on his work has been that of Edwin Muir.

Before he had met Muir, before he had accepted him as personal and artistic mentor, Brown had read Muir's *The Story and the Fable*, first published in 1940 when Brown was nineteen. In that book Muir had insisted that behind everyday events (the Story) lay an external extension of them (the Fable). Muir felt, for example, that his own idyllic Orkney childhood represented the fable of Eden; that his nightmarish experience in Glasgow (where his parents and two brothers died) represented the fable of the expulsion from Eden. Much as Plato had suggested that earthly events were imperfect copies of an abstract ideal, Muir claimed that fabulous archetypes determined the story of each individual life. The life of a man, Muir argued, was a particular example of the Life of Man. The eternal symbolic abstraction contained the essence of everyday existence.

Brown's artistic credo might be called the aesthetic Gospel According to Edwin Muir. Ordinary stories occur within an extraordinary and fabulous framework. The aesthetic gospel is most fully stated in Brown's novel *Magnus* (p. 140):

> there are constants in human nature, and constants in the human situation, and ... men in similar circumstances will behave roughly in the same fashion.
>
> Poetry, art, music thrive on these constants. They gather into themselves a huge scattered diversity of experience and reduce them to patterns; so that, for example, in a poem all voyages—past, present, and future—become The Voyage, and all battles The Battle, and all feats The Feast. This is to look at those events of time which resemble one another yet are never quite the same, in a symbolical way.

When you regard the world with such poetic intensity nothing is ever completely insignificant. It is this visionary approach that gives Brown's writing such a shining poetic quality. He never deviates from the vision: he consistently sees man as a superb anatomical model of an eternal idea. It is very Platonic, very Catholic, very Muiresque and very effective.

Although I have nothing but admiration for his poetry, I believe Brown's prose is more genuinely poetic than his verse. I do not mean what is normally thought of as "poetic prose"—great purple passages of romantic indulgence blanketing the vaguest, most ethereal narrative. I mean that he brings to prose a powerful structural presence and the linguistic riches we traditionally associate with poetry. Brown agrees:

First story that I thought good enough to be published was 'Tam'. . . . I'm hazy about my feelings at the time—perhaps it really *did* occur to me then (which I'm still inclined to believe) that I'm better at stories than poetry: more original, fresh—there's more of myself in my imaginative prose.

Surely this is because Brown needs a substantial spatial dimension in which to go beyond chronology to timelessness. His approach to the story is very musical, almost symphonic. He takes the seed of an idea and lets it grow organically until it is fully developed.

In the examination of Brown's work that follows we will see how he uses various characteristic techniques. There is the use of the multiple viewpoint so that the same event is seen from various angles. There is the use of counterpoint so that situations are enriched by ingenious juxtapositions. And there is this symphonic treatment of a story so that it grows organically from the seed of an idea to a great harvest of images. Technically, he is a brilliant writer, a master of his craft, a man with an impeccable control of form. There are also recognisable mannerisms: the fondness for the epithet "plangent", the frequent allusions to "seapinks". The thematic macrostructure of his work derives from the story-fable dichotomy; the many stylistic mannerisms contribute to the distinctive microstructure.

Most familiar of all his mannerisms is his reliance on the number seven. It counts as a telling feature in a large percentage of his work. It is not an arbitrary choice but is, as he says in *A Spell for Green Corn* (p. 25), "a good religious number". In the great traditional ballads that Brown admires seven is a magical number and there are seven sacraments, seven deadly sins, seven days in the creation in Genesis, seven stars in the astronomical Plough, while the five loaves and two fishes make seven. He also constantly refers to the biblical existence of a Seamless Garment, a symbol of almost impossible perfection. What I want to do in the following pages is show how George Mackay Brown weaves stylistic and thematic threads into the seamless garment of his writing.

2   Poet

It was as a poet that Brown first established his literary reputation
and his poetic work remains an important part of his total output,
though he has increasingly chosen to express himself in prose. He is a
versatile poet whose most obvious virtues are formal clarity and an
impressive command of verbal music. He has been influenced by the
inscape and sprung rhythms of Hopkins, by the ecclesiastical tone of
the later Eliot, by the metaphorical density of Dylan Thomas, by the
melancholy resignation (complete with refrain) and iconography
(complete with tinkers) of Yeats. He has three distinct styles in his
repertoire: a simple direct style, usually rhymed, which is employed
for contemporary themes; a measured style of great dignity,
normally in free verse, which simulates the saga voice; and a highly-
wrought intricately patterned ornamental style which deals with
ceremonial subjects.

Brown's fascination with literary forms has resulted in a wide
variety of stylistic effects. He can be sensuous in a thoroughly
contemporary manner; he can be stark and austere; he can expertly
imitate archaic forms. His immersion in the past has left him with a
fondness for runes and kennings. Runes, like the Norse examples in
Maes Howe, were statements cut in stone: doubtless the effort
involved accounts for their brevity. Brown has written a large
number of runic verses distinguished by sheer verbal compression.
Kennings were euphemistic metaphors employed by, among others,
the Icelandic skalds. Brown has revived rune and kenning in his
poems so that the Viking past is omnipresent in many of them. From
Scotland itself he has drawn heavily on the formal majesty and
dramatic intensity of the great traditional ballads.

Poetry is, basically, the most memorable form of literature and
there are many time-tested methods of achieving memorability. The
most readily apparent of these is rhyme and, when he wants to,
George Mackay Brown is adept at containing his natural fluency

within the strict patterns demanded by rhyme: *Loaves and Fishes*, for example, contains four sonnets—the most traditional of tight forms. Sometimes, too, Brown has a predeliction for internal rhymes as in 'Thorfinn' in *Loaves and Fishes*:

> Found an empty boat stuttering on the *rocks*
> And dawn-cold *cocks* cheering along the links.

or 'Sea Widow' in *Winterfold*:

> Another suggested a clover *ditch* for the drift of his seed ...
> That man was gray and gentle and *rich*.

With his affection for numbers and intricate patterns it is appropriate that Brown should experiment with rhyme by taking it to an extreme limit, by restricting himself to one basic rhyme in some poems. There is a ritualistic motive behind this, for in the "Resurrection" scene of his play *A Spell for Green Corn* Storm Kolson, the eternal fiddler, deliberately concentrates on a solitary assonantal rhyme (p. 61):

> Maskers, the spell that keeps pure the old rhyme of man DEATH BREAD BREATH. The tale of Everyman in three circling words—BREATH BREAD DEATH. A good fable, yea, for it is simple, passionate, inevitable, DEATH BREAD BREATH. So the generations rise and flourish and are cut down with this endless bourdon BREATH BREAD DEATH, surging monotones of corn.

Teresa, one of the seven women who narrate the finale of *Fishermen with Ploughs*, likewise favours the unity of rhyme (p. 90): 'I drew breath within a crude ballad, with only a few rhymes (grave-wave-weave: thorn-mourn-corn). . . . The ballad (earth-dearth-birth).' In two of the Ikey poems in *Fishermen with Ploughs* there is only one rhyme—'Ikey Crosses the Ward Hill' (where "hill" announces the single rhyme) and 'Ikey's Day' (where "hair" gives the rhyme). There are other examples but most impressive of all is 'Stations of the Cross' (which appears in *Fishermen with Ploughs*, *An Orkney Tapestry* and *Winterfold*) where there are fourteen rhymes—based on the opening "urn"—linking the couplets.

Such intricacy and ingenuity are evidence of consummate craftsmanship though Brown's poems are never only clever; we are never given the impression that the poems are a synthesis of literary devices for Brown is too emotionally involved in literature for that. Apart from his great love of alliteration, in fact, Brown is sparing in his use of rhetorical tricks. There are only four puns in his published work: "Euclidean light/*Ruled* the town" ('Hamnavoe', *Loaves and Fishes*), "The play was over" (Jane's first speech in *Fishermen with Ploughs*), "one door is a jar" ('The Sea', *Winterfold*), "the palm of a girl" (the Potter and Jar section of 'Stations of the Cross', *Winterfold*). His usually direct style also avoids irony with the massive exception of the poem 'Bjorn the Shetlander' in *Winterfold* where the speaker is ignorant of facts known to the reader.

What Brown excels at in his poems is the rhythm of speech, particularly the rhythm of Orkney speech. Orcadians speak in an inquisitive manner with a reversed cadence that begins on a low note and rises to a high one. It is full of pondered silences and Brown includes these in his poems; the pause between stanzas is an integral part of the total artistic execution. In *Greenvoe* (p. 15) Brown describes Orkney speech as "slow and wondering, like water lapping among stones", and this quality is apparent in his poetry. When he wants to present a voice from the past he adopts another voice, shot through with archaism, abstraction, and syntactical inversion, as in 'The Blind Helmsman' in *Fishermen with Ploughs*:

> Man goes, man voyages, into the blackest sun.
> Nor doth hero long keep
> Lithe limb or lissomness or laughter.
> Honey is bitter at last in the mouth.
> Fareth a shadow to the ghostly feast-halls.

Apart from the use of alliteration—where the liquidity of the 'l' sounds onomatopoetically suggest the surge of the sea—that opening is absolutely typical of Brown in that it announces the voyage theme that is basic to his approach. In this sense most of his poems have a strong narrative element—even his lyrics are going somewhere, taken up on a voyage from exile to home. He is not a first-personal poet—when an 'I' speaks it is usually in the context of a dramatic monologue. Nor is he a confessional poet (using the term, without religious connotations, to signify intimately autobiographical poetry); he seeks, rather, to express universal insights.

The Storm

Brown's first collection, *The Storm* (1954), was a local publication containing fourteen poems (and, given the fourteen stations of the cross, the number is important to the poet). Five of these poems were subsequently included in *Loaves and Fishes*: 'Dream of Winter', 'Saint Magnus on Egilshay', 'Gregory Hero' were substantially rewritten: 'Song: Further than Hoy' survived minus its penultimate stanza; 'The Exile' survived intact. The remaining nine poems show Brown quietly establishing his own poetic voice and his own iconography (Magnus yes, Knox no). 'The Prologue'—dated Newbattle, November 1952—is a declaration of intent:

> For Scotland I sing,
>   the Knox-ruined nation,
> that poet and saint
>   must rebuild with their passion.

The identity of the poet is obvious enough; the saint is Magnus who appears in the second poem 'The Road Home':

> The blessèd brave Saint Magnus
>   Who bowed his head and died.

That kind of unassimilated earnestness would be transformed, in Brown's later poetry, to something altogether less insistent. Persuasion would replace didacticism. The other poems largely elucidate the thematic shape of things to come. 'Song: Rognvald to Ermengarde' deals with the love-affair between the Orkney crusader and the Narbonne princess (used, strikingly, in 'Port of Venus' in *Loaves and Fishes*); 'Rackwick' is located in the "hidden valley of light" on Hoy that will provide the landscape for *Fishermen with Ploughs*; 'Chorus: Song Spring Will Come' and 'Death by Fire' are early attempts at dramatic writing; 'Orcadians: Seven Impromptus' comprises sketches of the sort of people who would later be treated to full-length portraits in the stories; 'The Tramp' is a tribute to the Orkney tinker ("he is a king of space") who will become the universal figure of Ikey (or Isaac or Jock) who figures as a witness to so many of the events in Brown's work.

The most interesting piece in *The Storm* is the title-poem whose opening is pure Hopkins:

> What blinding storm there was! How it
> Flashed with a leap and lance of nails,
> Lurching, O suddenly
> Over the lambing hills.

The use of enjambement carries the poem inexorably from storm to stillness; the storm-tormented voyager finds his feet at last as one of the monks of Eynhallow. The total impression suggested by *The Storm* is of a poet who knows exactly where he is going. He is determined to use verse as a vessel to take him from contemporary Stromness into the rich Orcadian past and back again. Because the vessel returns with a priceless cargo of ancient images Brown's poetry—like his prose—is able to transcend chronology and take readers into the fourth dimension of timelessness.

Loaves and Fishes

Loaves and Fishes appeared in 1959 and was Brown's first general introduction to the public. As he was thirty-eight when the book was published, it is not surprising that the collection represents no tentative beginning but a mature vision and a definite style. The vision has a strongly religious perspective which opens onto the mysteries of death and resurrection with which Brown is so preoccupied. Stylistically there are still debts to Hopkins, Muir, Yeats and Dylan Thomas yet the poetic voice is a sure one; its solemnity was utterly at odds with current literary fashion, (the domestic flatness of 'the Movement' had been established as orthodoxy in Robert Conquest's *New Lines* anthology of 1956) but the quiet concerned sincerity proved to be rich and rewarding. The book is arranged in three sections—nine poems in 'The Drowning Wave'; seven poems in 'Crofts Along the Shore'; nine poems in 'The Redeeming Wave'—and as the sequence of Brown's books is a crucial factor I will go through the book in the order he imposed on it.

The first poem, 'The Old Women' is one of the finest sonnets Brown has written; it has deservedly become an anthology-piece. It sounds, like a leitmotif, a theme that will recur again and again in his work, the theme of the wailing women. Following Muir's precept Brown always stresses the eternal Fable behind the everyday Story. So the wailing women are simultaneously real Orkney women and also reincarnations of the Daughters of Jerusalem, that 'great company of people, and of women, which also bewailed and lamented' Christ (*Luke* 23:27). In the poem the old women are presented as pier-head gossips. Confronted with the death of "a gray-eyed sober boy" they sing "An undersong of terrible holy joy". Though not a confirmed Catholic until 1961, Brown here exhibits a Christian consciousness. Every man dies in the sacrificial image of Christ. Jerusalem settles down in the street of Stromness.

'That Night in Troy', a poem in free verse about the aftermath of the sack of Troy, opens with "women ... trailing lamentation round the walls" so the weeping women are already familiar figures. Other figures are the girl in a hovel and the old philosopher whose bookish wisdom does not admit the disaster that surrounds him; these details give depth to the poem. The real point of it comes in a loving embrace between a man who has lost his brothers and a vestal virgin who has lost her virginity. Their spontaneous kiss, because of its promise of rebirth, "sealed a resurrection for the city". Conception and birth almost always conquer death in Brown's work. The poem ends with Ulysses beginning his odyssey to Ithica with a premonition of Penelope.

Another sonnet, 'The Death of Peter Esson', laments the death of a Stromness man who was tailor, town librarian, and an elder of the Free Kirk (an extreme Calvinist sect of the Church of Scotland). A righteous dislike of presbyterianism permeates Brown's writing and he often describes the wanton destruction of Roman Catholic images at the time of the Reformation (the story 'Father Halcrow, Priest' in *A Calendar of Love* is an example). This sonnet, though, is a touching tribute to an old friend (whose "seventieth rock was near") dying certain he was one of the Calvinist elect ("The predestined needle quivered on the mark"). The theme of man dying at seventy (*seven* decades, notice: the biblical threescore years and ten) is repeated in 'The Masque of Bread' in which the dead man seeks an answer in the afterlife. For Brown the spectacle of bread being brought forth from the earth to nourish men, like Christ's body, is a potent symbol of resurrection majestically stated in this poem which, like 'That Night in Troy', is written in conversationally pitched verse that hovers round the iambic pentameter. The religious symbolism of seedtime and harvest is stated, more directly, in the landscape 'December Day, Hoy Sound'.

So far we have met the weeping women and considered the resurrection of the corn. In 'Thorfinn' we have an early example of his use of Viking history. The historical Thorfinn was, as we know from the *Orkneyinga Saga*, the strongest of all the Orkney earls. Before his death in 1065 on the tidal island, the Brough of Birsay, he had ruthlessly hammered together a unified earldom. In Brown's poem we have a timeless Thorfinn wandering, anachronistically, in a land where "every casual car was the Black Maria". Like any Orkney fisherman he drowns—though his descent is also through a sea of images and a surfeit of alliteration (with "dawn-cold cocks cheering along the links"). After a glimpse of his own 'Themes' (they're all there—the tinkers, the resurrection of the corn, the weeping women, the ploughmen) Brown reverses the method of 'Thorfinn'. In that poem an Orkney Earl died the death of an ordinary fisherman; in 'Gregory Hero' a typical Orkney fisherman dies dramatically like a Norse warrior ("he was/A Viking ship, a white stallion").

The first section of the book ends, as it began, with a sonnet. In 'Port of Venus' the hero is another Viking, Rognvald Kolson ("The holy earl") who is remembered for founding St Magnus Cathedral in 1137 and for beginning a pilgrimage to Jerusalem in 1151. The first landfall of the Viking crusaders was Narbonne, in the south of France, where the prince of the city turned out to be a woman, Countess Ermengarde, with whom Rognvald fell in love. In the poem she is "a girl with snooded hair/And shy cold breasts". I believe poems like this should have an explanatory note by Brown. The reader ignorant of the historical Ermengarde (and it is unfair to take for granted a general knowledge of Orkney's history) would be puzzled by the reference to "their prince, a girl". Even Edwin Muir, an Orkneyman and a poet, failed to catch the allusion for in a letter of 29 April 1958 to Mrs Norah Smallwood of The Hogarth Press he said "['Port of Venus'] is about an incident in the life of St Magnus, the Orkney saint".*

* I am grateful to Mrs Smallwood for showing me a copy of this letter.

The second part of the book, 'Crofts Along the Shore', begins with a rhymed poem (*abacdedec*) in which a simple narrative has the force of a legend. Apart from the Yeatsian refrain in the second line of each stanza, 'The Stranger' is very much all Brown's own work in that it uses the triple viewpoint (cf. 'A Treading of Grapes' in *A Time to Keep*) to give three angles on the same object. The information explored in the poem is that a stranger has begged food and lodging at a poor house and has repaid this by making the daughter of the house pregnant. The mother finds the stranger "A poet or a prince"; the daughter dotes on his child; the father—who suspects the stranger was "a tink"—admits his coming transformed his wife and daughter. The reader is left with the possibility that the stranger was an angel: such unexpected miracles are commonplace occurrences in Brown's writing. 'The Stranger' is followed by the delightful 'Childsong', a mother's lullaby for a child.

One of the greatest poems Brown has published is, in my opinion, 'Hamnavoe'. This is a moving tribute to his father who was born and died in Stromness; a posthumous gift of images to a father whose "gay poverty ... kept/My seapink innocence/From the worm and black wind". The poem is a portrait of one day in the life of Hamnavoe (Stromness) and comprises a steady accumulation of marvellously vivid images so that the people of the town come to life:

> A tinker keened like a tartan gull
> At cuithe-hung doors. A crofter lass
> Trudged through the lavish dung
> In a dream of cornstalks and milk.

More than that, the town itself seems alive with incident, glorying in its "pipe-spitting pier-head", its "ignorant closes", its "kirk, in a gale of psalms", its "tumult of roofs". The universe, too, becomes a familiar part and parcel of the little seaport, for the moon hangs like a "buttered bannock". Through this world Brown's postman father voyages with stops to deliver his "penny letters". The felicitious details and rhythmic fluency enable Brown to wrap up the town in a cosy parcel of images so he can deliver them to his father. Normally when Brown uses quatrains they are rhymed and accentual and self-contained (as in the song 'Stars' that comes after 'Hamnavoe').

Here the verse is more open with the first stanza's syllabic count of 10.12.6.6. setting a pattern for the remaining eleven stanzas. The use of enjambement allows the first three quatrains to flow into each other; the voyage begins with a surge.

So far the poems in *Loaves and Fishes* have been rather solemn and melancholy. The satirical approach of 'The Death Bird' offers some diversity. The poem is in two contrasted parts both dealing with a man's death. The first death is celebrated by an expensive funeral. A local bigwig, Knarston, has died. For him the lark—a symbol of beauty—is silent. Instead "A bird/Winged with fivers" shrieks at his funeral, a theatrical event with mourners acting out their simulated grief. Knarston will not be missed. However when, in the second part, the drunken Peero dies under the stars he has no flowers or tears but "over the corn/A lark sang". For Brown the man who indulges his senses is worth more than the man who carves out a career. The sensual man who claims to have heard the lark sing for Peero is Halcro who gets the following poem, 'Halcro', to himself. He is near to death but uninterested in pious words of comfort. He prefers news of the world he has lived in, a world of brawling men and beautiful women. As the sixth, and final, quatrain tells us such news moves him:

> Then see his bone-bright hands
> Frail on the chair, grown firm again
> In the stillness of old brawls,
> Torn nets, sweet dust, and tangled grain.

This central section of the book closes with 'The Lodging', a poem on the subject of Christ's nativity. It is a strangely flat poem that relies too much on biblical images without reworking them; there are simply references to "The Roman in a strange land", the indifferent innkeeper, the "queer pair" in the byre. Yet the event it obliquely deals with ("The cry from the byre") is the greatest single moment celebrated in Brown's work.

The religious element really comes into its own in the final section of the book, 'The Redeeming Wave'. It starts with a ballad, 'The Heavenly Stones'. The speaker is the young Christ who is offered tempting gifts by the three wise men. The allegorical extension of the biblical incident confers abstract overtones on the gifts. The gold (worldly wealth) Christ sinks in a midden; the sweet-smelling frankincense (sensuality) he throws on the floor; the bitter myrrh (sacrifice) he reluctantly drinks. Christ appears as 'The Exile' in the next poem, a set of eight quatrains inspired by the Sermon on the Mount:

> His hammer heart
> Thuds in his breast
> 'What Love devises,
> That is best'.

It manages to convey the stark simplicity of Christ's message. In 'Dream of Winter' Christ is "the victim nailed against the night . . . the hooded victim, broken to let men live". The iambic pentameters present Christ's death as winter, his resurrection as spring. The four seasons are treated symbolically, as well as realistically, in Brown's poems and stories.

With Brown's biblical poems the reader is on familiar territory; the images have become part of Western consciousness. To re-awaken the images Brown has recourse to ingenious variations. In Magnus, the martyred earl of Orkney, he has his own indigenous saint. 'Saint Magnus on Egilsay', a rewritten version of the poem of the same name in *The Storm*, presents Magnus as an elemental force able to work miracles of fertility. The poem opens with one of Brown's classic images, the plough amorously penetrating the virgin earth to make it fertile enough to sustain life. Only Egilsay resisted this agricultural embrace, the poem argues, until Magnus was martyred there, "a broken saint". In the *Orkneyinga Saga* (Taylor's translation, p. 211) Egilsay is overcome with fertility following the death of Magnus: "The spot before was moss-grown and stony; but shortly after, the worth of Earl Magnus shone so bright before God that there grew green swards where he was slain". Brown makes poetry out of this legend:

> Root, stalk, and flower
> Twined in a riot through the acre of death
> And larks cut lyrical nests deep in its turf.

The beautifully shaped—around a rhyme-scheme of *abcdcead*—formal 'Elegy' begins with "Magnustide long swords of rain" and the ritual of the plough:

25

> The ploughman turns
> Furrow by holy furrow
> The liturgy of April.

(The metaphor owes something to Dylan Thomas: cf. "the parables of sun light", 'Poem in October'.) The poem was written, Brown told me, about "a young woman who died in childbirth—she was a beautiful singer, and also a promising poet". The seed is stubborn because of the girl's death yet, bending the tragedy to the truth of his images, Brown sees her burial as a prelude to resurrection in "Cornstalks, golden conspirators" that will renew her as "immortal bread".

A more enigmatic mood prevails in 'The Shining Ones' in which Christ, or someone Christlike, seeks the gateway to eternity. The dead man is never positively identified but the account of his boxing match at an Orkney fair could well be taken as a modern counterpart of Christ's encounter with Judas:

> He fought Young Kelly in the Lammas booth
> (The surgeon's scar still vivid on his side)
> Stayed his three rounds, and won his thirty bob.

Brown's habitual symbolism suggests that nothing created by him is only a Story; the Fable is always near at hand. As he says in the charming 'Song: Further than Hoy', "Further than history/the legends thicken".

One crude legend that Brown subscribes to is that Knox, and Knox alone, was the ruination of Scotland's spiritual potential. In his 'Scotland 1941' Edwin Muir had written of a paradisal Scotland, full of "busy corn-fields", that survived idyllically until "Knox and Melville clapped their preaching palms". Personally I would have thought that Brown could have found some sympathy for Knox who was, after all, a peasant's son who had the courage to defy the divine right of a Catholic monarch. Still, in the sonnet 'Chapel Between Cornfield and Shore'—inspired by the fact that in the old graveyard of Stromness there are a few pieces of wall that might be the remains of a Catholic chapel—Brown accuses Knox:

> Above the ebb, that gray uprooted wall
> Was arch and chancel, choir and sactuary,

A solid round of stone and ritual.
Knox brought all down in his wild hogmanay.

The sestet of the sonnet is a prayer for the restoration of the spirit of the conjectural chapel.

Loaves and Fishes closes with 'Daffodils' in which three daffodils are symbolically transformed into "Three Marys at the cross". Because the daffodils flourish in March (like harbingers of the harvest), because they die before midsummer ("perish before the rose/bleeds on the solstice stone") Brown sees the floral trinity as

Mary Mary and Mary
triangle of grief.

The Year of the Whale

The Year of the Whale (1965) is a much more morbid collection than *Loaves and Fishes*: it opens and closes with a funereal poem (the first about an Orkney fisherman, the last about the death of John F. Kennedy) and in between are poems about death and its alternatives—love and faith. The first poem in the book, 'The Funeral of Ally Flett', is a remarkable technical achievement. It embodies rich pattern and stanzaic complexity. There are seven eight-line stanzas rhyming *abcacdbd* and conforming (with a couple of exceptions) to a syllabic count of 8.4.8.4.10.4.10.8. The feeling, though, is not syllabic but accentual—the penultimate line of each stanza being an iambic pentameter ("And every loveliest lilt must have a close"). Each stanza comprises a complete sentence, opening with a reason (all but one stanza begins "Because . . .") and ending with the name or rank of a mourner. Despite this complicated structure Brown achieves a simple elegiac effect and imparts solid information about the dead man: his youth, his sexual timidity, the season of his death ("the scythe was in the oats"), his occupation, his friendliness, the tragedy of a short life.

This poem prepares us for more death. 'Shipwreck' describes the fate of seven men from the sinking ship, the *Maggi*. Paul is rescued by milkmaids; Jan is found dead with tobacco in his teeth; Gregory's body is eaten by crabs; Robin is cast up by the sea; Peero dies with his little political ambitions; Peter returns to read his own tombstone; Donald dies at sixteen.

It is surprising how much life there is in elongated free verse about such a deadly subject: in any fishing community death is an occupational hazard. The death of the Scottish clan system in 1746 is recounted in 'Culloden'. It is narrated by a Drumnakeil man who kills an English soldier (echoing Owen's poem 'Strange Meeting') and dreams of a reunion with his Penelope (Morag): "Weaving, she sings of the beauty of defeat".

Faith is the antidote to death and defeat in Brown's work and there are three consecutive monastic poems in *The Year of the Whale*. On the tidal island, the Brough of Birsay, the ruins of a twelfth-century chapel stand on the foundations of a seventh-century Celtic church: the sort of architectural evidence of antiquity that Brown delights in. This Celtic settlement is reconstructed in 'Horseman and Seals'. The trusting monks build a boat so that, even when the tide is in, visitors will be able to come to the island. A horseman shouts to them; twenty seals "with their beautiful gentle old men's faces" listen to a psalm. The world is made totally secure through faith. The first stanza of the poem shows how Brown conveys endurability by ending each line, firmly, with a noun. 'The Abbot' is a more contrived poem telling of the soothing impact of religion on seven robust men. 'Our Lady of the Waves' is set in Eynhallow, site of a twelfth-century monastery. It is ritualistic to the point of dogmatism because the reader is asked to believe that he who asks shall receive as long as he prefaces his request with a prayer to "a figure of Our Lady".

It seems to me that Brown is merely going through the motions in his dogmatic poems. They depend so much on sheer faith that the poet feels little need actively to engage the attention of the reader. He is content to offer a recitation of a supposedly heavenly situation, a litany. To create poetry—to conjure verbal magic, that is—out of verse, the words themselves have to carry conviction so far that they move the reader along with them. Brown admits this in 'The Poet'. When the poet, a "blind lyrical tramp", goes among the people with his mask and his cloak and his guitar he spreads happiness. This, Brown implies, is merely a sideshow, a peacock display. The real task of poetry is something more intense, infinitely more difficult: it is the "interrogation of silence".

To counterpoint the three monastic poems Brown has a trio of geriatric poems. 'Farm Labourer' is spoken by seventy-year-old

Ward in two stanzas rhyming *abcaddbc*. The old man is weary after a lifetime of resurrecting "Bread and ale out of the skinflint corn"; there is an implied self-criticism in this for Brown realises that the men who do the work in the fields see it as a struggle, not in symbolic terms. 'Old Fisherman with Guitar' is likewise in two stanzas (rhyming *abcacb*). The old man's entire life seems to be shrunk down to his hands, his withered fingers plucking at a guitar; the same hands, the poet tells us, were once strong enough to cut a drowned corpse from a net and gather the mouth of a woman to his mouth. The title poem, 'The Year of the Whale', laments the passing of old men who are snuffed out like candles during the winter. In three stanzas skilfully rhymed *abcdecbFade* (with F serving as an inter-stanzaic rhyme) the narrator expresses concern that the memory of the "great whale year" is fading away. The poignancy of old age is its stark contrast with the vigour of youth, for all the narrators in the three geriatric poems have been physically robust young men. The remembrance of things past is all that matters to the old and in the title-poem the memory is of heroic proportions for there had been a bad harvest,

> Then whale by whale by whale
>> Blundering on the rock with its red stain
>>> Crammed our winter cupboards with oil and meat.

As usual the image gains strength from its functional importance to the people. The images are rooted in reality.

Things take a lighter turn in 'Trout Fisher' (a two-stanza poem rhyming *abcbdadcb*) in which the fisherman does a Judas on the fish by selling his "subtle loch-craft" to tourists for pieces of silver. After a little tribute to 'The Twelve Piers of Hamnavoe' there is a fine processional poem on 'Hamnavoe Market'. Naturally there are seven men and naturally their outing becomes a collective odyssey. This is the poem, it seems to me, where Brown most successfully simulates the natural speech-rhythms of Orkney, the inquisitive, halting, step-by-step delivery:

> Grieve bought a balloon and a goldfish.
> He swung through the air.
> He fired shotguns, rolled pennies, ate sweet fog from a stick.

29

Here there is no cunning rhyme-scheme; the natural flow of the language is enough to make the poem memorable. It reads and sounds like a story expertly told by a seasoned raconteur in a pub, complete with the punchline about the fallen, drunken Johnston:

> They drove home from the Market under the stars
> Except for Johnston
> Who lay in a ditch, his mouth full of dying fires.

'Country Girl' and 'Boy from the Shore' are two linked love-poems. In the first poem Brown employs a favourite symbol, the completion contained in a circle. Naming seven circles the poem leads lyrically to the final and most intimately human one, for the man holds his girl "in the hot unbroken circle of my arms". 'Boy from the Shore' presents the triumph of love over local gossip.

Seven metaphors for the climate are offered in 'Weather Bestiary' and in 'The Hawk' Brown depicts seven days in the life of a hawk. For Brown the hawk is a symbol of violent death; while the dove symbolises (as it does in most cultures) peace. Like Ted Hughes, Brown admires the sheer functional precision of predatory animals: they are dedicated to killing. Brown's hawk falls like a curse on chickens and blackbirds, rabbits and rats. It too, though, has to die,

> And on Saturday he fell on Bigging
> And Jock lowered his gun
> And nailed a small wing over the corn.

Compared to the verbal precision of 'The Hawk' the rhetorical injunctions in 'The Image in the Hills' fall flat. Brown is not an intellectual poet; his work is carried along not by an overtly cerebral process but by intuitively experienced images and symbols. 'The Image in the Hills' contains too many orders to his muse. In an anti-Progress poem, 'The Condemned Well', Brown trades his symbolic expertise for an opportunity to make an assertion. The well is old, it has quenched many thirsts, but it will disappear and a poetic part of life with it. The punchline, when it comes, does not diminish Progress; it displays pique:

> Fool, thou poet,
> Tomorrow is the day of the long lead pipe.

It is perhaps unjust to cite a weak poem when there are so many fine ones around it. The level of Brown's work is consistently superb so that one lapse makes hardly a dent in the total artistic edifice. A master of the ballad metre, Brown's 'The Sailor, the Old Woman, and the Girl' has a darkly humorous atmosphere. The sailor, tormented by lust, asks an old woman for advice. She suggests that when he is tempted by the girl's youth he should "use the black worm of the mind" and realise that one day she will be an old hag herself. That intimation of mortality is enough for the sailor who voyages onwards to the rhythm of the ballad:

> The girl sang from another shore
> And the tranced oars beat on,
> And the old woman's fingers went
> Like roots through the gray stone.

The influence of Yeats is apparent in 'Harald, the Agnostic Ale-Drinking Shepherd' in which the eponymous hero condemns both papist and protestant and decides to keep to his ale when he is not watching over his flock. In 'The Mirabel' three old men lament "a boat of small luck" and the fact that weeping women can be distracted by baubles. Along with fishermen and crofters, and monks and Vikings, the most familiar figures in Brown's poems are tinkers. The commonest tinker in the poems is an archetypal figure called Ikey and he—one of Brown's enduring creations—speaks in 'Ikey on the People of Hellya'. Ikey is motivated by greed and when he is rebuffed he turns nasty (putting his knife in the net of a fisherman who rebuked him). He is man at his most animal level.

The penultimate poem in *The Year of the Whale*, 'Fisherman and Boy', consists of fatherly advice from an old man to a young boy. First, the lad is to avoid death by drowning, drinking, soldiering, womanising, suicide; second, he is to control his lust and look to his fishing boat; third, he is to realise that Orkney is an autonomous world in itself. For there is Birsay, where Magnus was born and buried; the grandiose countours of Hoy; Egilsay where Magnus was martyred; the standing stones of Stenness; St Magnus Cathedral in Kirkwall where Magnus's skull was found. If the boy stays in his native land he will be contented, for

> you will learn more in Orkney
> Than Mansie did
> Who made seven salt circles of the globe.

That, at any rate, has been Brown's own experience.

The last poem, 'The Seven Houses', is dedicated to the memory of President John F. Kennedy who was assassinated in Dallas on 22 November 1963. As a Roman Catholic, Brown must have felt the impact of Kennedy's death keenly. However the poem does not really manage to convey his emotions. It is a purely occasional poem (using the term, as Goethe did, to describe a poem written for a special occasion). Man—and Kennedy embodies mankind's hopes in the poem—goes through seven doors: to the House of the Womb, the House of Birth, the House of Man, the House of Corn and Grape, the House of Love, the House of Policy and the House of History. Apart from the observation that "In growing darkness, you lit one lamp" the poem relies on platitudes and is one of the weakest pieces Brown has published. Judging from 'The Seven Houses' Brown's muse does not extend beyond the islands of Orkney.

Fishermen with Ploughs

Fishermen with Ploughs (1971) is set on the Orkney island of Hoy, in the valley of Rackwick. It is Brown's only attempt so far at the long poem though, by choosing a sequential form rather than continuous narrative, what we are given is a series of interdependent poems. In *An Orkney Tapestry*, Brown devotes a chapter to Rackwick and describes the desolation of the place (p. 28):

> The poignant thing about this beautiful valley ("the bay of wreckage") is that ... it has been utterly abandoned. The floor of the valley and its fertile western slope are littered with half-ruined crofts—the windows blind, the roofs fallen in, the hearth-stones forever black. Here and there among the barns and outhouses are stone jars, rusted ploughs, broken cups. There was abundant life in Rackwick once; the life ebbed out rapidly through some flaw; the place is full of the ghosts of centuries.

In 1952 only two young people, brothers, remained among the old folk of the valley. They drowned while playing on a raft in Rackwick's burn. The valley had finally died. Now the valley attracts tourists and artists: the composer Peter Maxwell Davies (who has set Brown's Rackwick lyric 'The Stations of the Cross' and written an opera *The Martyrdom of St Magnus* to words by Brown) has settled in the croft of Bunertoon. Still, tragic memories pervade the place.

It is customary in a long poem to introduce a struggle between good and evil. Brown's hero is the valley itself; his villain is his old enemy Progress, "a cancer that makes an elemental community look better, and induces a false euphoria, while it drains the life out of it remorselessly" (*An Orkney Tapestry*, pp. 50–1). In a prefatory note to the sequence Brown introduces the villain, Progress, and states his argument that "the quality of life grows poorer as Progress multiplies its gifts on a simple community". This is a dubious premise—for without Progress people are at the mercy of natural disaster and disease—but Brown builds the poem on it. As well as the notion of Progress, Brown relies on the abstraction Fate so that the mechanics of the sequence operate within a deterministic world; the tragedy of Rackwick has an inevitability about it. Individuals are not blamed for the fate that befalls Rackwick, they simply succumb to the unavoidable tidal wave of Progress. This gives the poem a pessimistic atmosphere, a melancholy climate.

The opening section of the poem, Dragon and Dove, describes the settlement of Rackwick in the ninth century by a tribe of Norse fishermen. In Norway the tribe have been attacked by the Dragon (a poetic synonym for natural disaster) and seek salvation in a voyage. The first poem, 'Building the Ship', describes the construction of the ship *Dove* (with its titular promise of peace). Using all his linguistic resources Brown conveys the sense of period by resuscitating the alliterative manner of Old English poetry:

> Men daylaboured, were dappled with lanterns.
> They beat design on the thwart timbers.
> Loomed a dry dove from June leafage.
> That bird would unlock the horizon westwards.

As each line carries the burden of a complete sentence Brown establishes a mood of caution: each step has to be carefully considered for every decision has a terrible finality. The *Dove* takes seven months to build.

The next two poems—'The Fight With the Dragon' and 'The Death of Thorkeld'—tell how the tribal chief, Thorkeld, died in his battle against the Dragon of natural disaster. He is succeeded by his son Njal. On the instructions of Fate ('The Blind Helmsman') Njal is told to forsake fishing for agriculture and to make his woman, Gudrun, the mother of harvesters. The fertile soil of Rackwick is to be amorously probed by the plough; Gudrun, a human seed-jar, is to receive Njal's seed. This is the rise of Rackwick. By making almost every line an independent unit, a complete sentence, Brown has suggested the precarious nature of the settlement of the valley. Only in the last poem in the section, 'Whales', does the poet offer a feeling of exhilaration. The Norse tribe, after all, have come to a new place and have adopted a new way of life (crofting taking priority over fishing). The whales come to them like magnificent gifts from the sea; the whales are described in a series of metaphors, "threshing lumps,/Blue hills, cartloads of thunder ... tons of love ... floating feast-halls". Rackwick's beautiful valley has embraced the Norse voyagers; they have escaped the Dragon and found a new home.

The language changes completely for the four poems in section two, 'Our Lady'. Having successfully settled in the valley the tribe have taken bread and ale from the soil. In order to round out their existence, to dignify their lives with a profound reason for living, Brown brings them to an imaginary chapel in the fields (most likely there *was* a chapel at Rackwick before the Reformation but nothing remains). Because the life of a crofter is a hard one that involves sacrifice Brown's 'Stations of the Cross' draws a striking comparison between the life of Christ and the life of the crofter. He regards this poem with special affection: "A poem called 'Stations of the Cross' in which Christ's passion is counterpointed with the work of the crofter is I think a key poem for anyone who is interested in my writings."[*] The poem consists of fourteen couplets, one for each station of the cross. Each couplet has one long and one short line:

> Scythes are sharpened to bring you down,
> King Barleycorn.

[*] *Chapman*, vol. iv., no. 4., summer 1976, p. 23.

The couplets are linked by the single rhyme that ends each short line:
urn/turn/born/burn/borne/yarn/thorn/mourn/corn/torn/quern/
horn/bairn/barn. In the poem, primitive agricultural life is given a
weighty Christian symbolism; the grinding of corn, for example, is a
crucifixion:

> The fruitful stones thunder around,
> Quern on quern.

Christ thus becomes an essential part of the crofters' existence—he is
no impossibly distant divinity but a "rapt bairn".

Strengthened with this religion the fishermen with ploughs act out
their lives under the statue of Our Lady ('A Jar of Salt', 'The Statue
in the Hills') and when they take to the sea again ('Helmsman') for
an occasional voyage a Bishop is always on Board. It is a basic
existence made beautiful, so Brown believes, by faith. As he says in
An Orkney Tapestry (p. 36) "Life went on that way for centuries in
Rackwick. Birth, love, labour, death—this was the rhythm of the
crofter-fisherman's life, generation after generation".

In the third section of the sequence, 'Hall and Kirk', three
centuries are spanned: we take in the witch-burning of the sixteenth
century and end with the war against Napoleonic France. The
Reformation has cast a black shadow over the beautiful valley; it is a
time of guilt and accusation. The poor crofters suffer at the hands of
the lairds, the taxmen and the press-gangs. In 'Witch' old Wilma is
taken from her croft, Greenhill, to be burned at Gallowsha; "the
black music" ('A Reel of Seven Fishermen') is making a mockery of
the simple faith of the people. And always the horsemen come with
their insistent demands for rent ('Taxman') and service ('Grave
Stone') and soldiers ('Buonaparte, the Laird, and the Volunteers').
Decay and death are settling in Rackwick ('Shroud') and even
Ikey's anarchic behaviour is scrutinised by legalistic minds—he is (in
'Sheriff of Orkney Contra Ikey') taken to Kirkwall for a public
whipping. The language in this section is terse and cryptic; the voice
of the people is being stifled as the grip of Calvinism tightens round
their throats.

Eighteen poems make up 'Foldings', the fourth section. The
Victorian age has ostensibly liberated the valley people: the Scottish
Education Act of 1872 has made them literate, the Crofters' Act of

1886 has given them a measure of security. In 'The Laird' the speaker laments the passing of his power:

> I'd quit this withered heraldry
> To drive with Jock in his cart
>   To the hill for peat.

And in 'Crofter's Death' the speaker realises the people "will leave this keening valley". Meanwhile the crofter-fishermen try to make the best of their difficult world, ploughing the soil and fishing the sea ('Then Four Great Angels', 'Black Furrow, Gray Furrow') and pulling the peat from the earth ('Peat Cutting'). Always they are close to death: in 'A Winter Bride' Jock is drowned; in 'Homage to Heddle' a once-vigorous man reads his bible while waiting for death; in 'New Year Stories' the dead are summoned from "silent kirkyards"; in 'Twins' there is a double death; in 'A Warped Boat' Willag drowns; in 'Funeral' there is a communal mourning; in 'Foldings' women become widows; in 'Jock' the death of the valley is anticipated:

> Crofts lie strewn, transfigured wrecks
> In a fenceless sea.

Throughout this section, Ikey alone is fit to survive among decay for his trade is scavenging ('Ikey Crosses the Ward Hill') when the doors of the crofts are closed to him ('Ikey's Day'). There is still the odd bonus of whales from the sea ('Ploughman and Whales') but life on Rackwick promises little ('Fiddlers at the Wedding'). Between birth and death there is fishing and crofting and the sweetness of women; or, to put the same thing poetically, as Brown does in his prose poem 'A Jar of Honey',

> Between [the gate of life] and the dark gate were the fish and
> the fleece and the loaf, the oil jars and the jars of salt and the
> jars of grain, and the one small jar of honey.

In nineteen poems the fifth part, 'The Stone Hawk', utters the curse of Progress that has crippled the valley. We have arrived in the twentieth century and the young people of Rackwick don the drab uniform of modern city life ('Love Letter'):

The croft girls are too young.
Nothing but giggles, lipstick, and gramophone records.

Life in the valley is becoming more ardous: the 'Haddock Fishermen' are left to "probe emptiness all the afternoon" while 'The Laird's Falcon', a heraldic symbol of death, flies over the valley. Almost as ominous as the falcon is the drab presbyterian religion. The fisherman has become a kirk elder ('Sea Runes'):

> Charlag who has read the prophets
> A score of times
> Has thumbed the salt book also, wave after wave.

And the crofter had become a kirk elder ('Hill Runes'):

> Andrew who has read the gospel
> Two or three times
> Has quizzed the clay book also, furrow by furrow.

And Ikey the tinker can expect only cold charity from these people ('Beachcomber'):

> Sunday, for fear of the elders,
> I sit on my bum.

Over the cornfields, like a parody of the crucifixion, stands 'The Scarecrow in the Schoolmaster's Oats' while a child observes that people come, not in friendship, but with ornithological interests, "Strangers ... With cameras, binoculars, bird books" ('A Child's Calendar'). The people no longer rely on the sea ('Windfall') or the soil ('Girl') or the old faith ('Old Man'), but gather round the shop ('Roads') for "loaves, sugar, paraffin, newspapers, gossip" or rely on the van to provide them with "jam, sugar, tea, paraffin" ('Butter') or patent medicine ('The Coward'). Progress brings not only convenient provisions but a war more terrible than any Viking raid ('Sabbath'):

> That was the year of the submarine.
> Men sank and burned.
> Women turned slowly to stone.

Still the wind sweeps over the heads of the people ('The Big Wind') and still there is the promise of rebirth in an island wedding ('Fisherman's Bride'). But in 1952 two brothers, the last of the young people left in the valley, drown in the burn ('The Drowning Brothers'); the same burn that, littered with progressive rubbish, "carries the valley filth/Out to the seven brightnesses of the bay". The final poem in the fifth section, 'Dead Fires', gives a picture of utter desolation, the empty crofts as cold as the kirk:

> The poor and the good fires are all quenched.
> Now, cold angel, keep the Valley
> From the bedlam and cinders of A Black Pentecost.

The final section of the sequence—the three-part 'Return of the Women'—is (save for eighteen lines of poetry) entirely in prose, a set of dramatic monologues. Modern civilisation has been destroyed by a new Dragon of disaster—The Black Flame. This holocaust wipes out technology and the survivors are left to their own resources though they have lost touch with the elements. Seven women and six men escape, in the boat *The Truelove*; Saul the Skipper is their natural leader. Apart from an old nurse Bianca, the odd-woman-out, the men and women form pairs: Jane, the blind schoolteacher, and Siegfried; Natasha, a violinist, and Conrad; Sophie, a ballet-dancer, and David; Teresa, a convent-girl, and Simon; fifteen-year-old Marilyn and John. Each of the women speak once in the three parts of this final section.

The disaster itself is presented "off-stage", as it were, through pun and irony. Jane recalls a classroom play about the Sack of Troy (a reference back to 'That Night in Troy' in *Loaves and Fishes*). A freckled girl plays Helen while "Hector astride a desk brandished his ruler", then (p. 81),

> Far too soon, Troy began to burn.... Fire bowed through the door, a mad inspector.... The play was over.

The play was over: the classroom play was at an end, like laughter in the world. In Teresa's first monologue she remembers observing Roman Catholic rituals ironically aware that an immediate man-made tragedy is about to occur (p. 84):

The Gospel was parables and miracles in Galilee; we were there at the roadside, watching, listening, wondering. . . . Soon men are going to commit their wickedest worst crime yet, the murder of God.

The memories fade in this part, 'Landfall', as the survivors approach Rackwick with "the sack of seed corn" (p. 82).

In the second part, 'Houses', the survivors settle in seven abandoned Rackwick crofts. It is seedtime. They find (p. 89) that "one old plough rusting in the bog" becomes "brighter than The Plough in the January sky". A remnant of Progress, on the other hand, the tractor, is worse than useless. This is an allusion to Muir's 'The Horses' in which "The tractors lie about our fields. . . . We leave them where they are and let them rust" for Sophie gives what amounts to a prose paraphrase of Muir's poem (p. 89):

> Well, one day when David was among the hills didn't two horses cross the heather towards him, very delicate and shy [Muir has "Stubborn and shy"], shaggy garrons. . . . And at last the mare came right up to him and fitted her skull into his warm welcoming hand.

At the beginning of the final part, 'Harvest', we find that (p. 93) "All the women are in different stages of pregnancy" except for the barren witness Bianca. She suspects that Saul the Skipper is responsible for it all (p. 94):

> Saul is the master here, he has one aim, to fill the valley with a torrent of his own goats. To him the women are nothing but walking wombs, seed jars.

Saul is, in fact, asserting his authority with mindless brutality. He orders Siegfried to be the shepherd, he knocks Conrad down in the cornfield, he ritually flogs John so he will become a beachcomber. He has assumed too much authority by being "patriarch, law-giver, priest, keeper of seed, measurer of the west, laird" (p. 99). He has been contaminated by Progress.

The survivors come to grief in Rackwick. They do not respond to a priceless discovery, the old statue of Our Lady; the crop fails because, according to Saul the Skipper, "The Black Flame scorched the seed" (p. 98); Jane's baby dies. In their makeshift Harvest Home they pass round a solitary jar of ale. The Skipper bans the word "corn" and decrees that the survivors will henceforth make their living from the sea. Eleven centuries before them a Norse tribe had turned from fishing to crofting and fertilised the beautiful valley; the survivors will turn from crofting to fishing. The final sentence of the whole sequence tells us that the survivors have "returned, uncaring, into the keeping of the Dragon".

Poems New and Selected

Fishermen with Ploughs is an impressive achievement, though in laying so much stress on the decline and fall of the valley of Rackwick, Brown has neglected to show us in what way the life there was once so idyllic (unless we are expected to believe that the open worship of Our Lady is the supreme happiness). Each poem gains contextual strength from the overall concept, through the poems still retain a considerable measure of autonomy: Brown values concision in his poems as much as gradual expansion in his stories. *Fishermen with Ploughs* was quickly followed by *Poems New and Selected* (1971) which contains fifteen poems from *Loaves and Fishes*, twenty-one poems from *The Year of the Whale* and thirteen new poems. (The book-jacket claims fourteen new poems but one of them, 'Our Lady of the Waves', had already appeared in *The Year of the Whale* and only one line is altered—"Well he carries word and wine for the priest" becomes "Well he brings wine and word to the priest"— imperceptibly.) 'Three Songs from a Play' consists of two ballads and a lyric from *A Spell for Green Corn* and these are cited in the fourth chapter of this book.

'The Five Voyages of Arnor' is a last testament, in free verse, of a dying poet. In the *Orkneyinga Saga*, Arnor Earl's skald, an eleventh century poet has twenty-two poems; Brown's poem is an original composition that manages to duplicate the assertive tone of the historical Arnor. He has made four voyages out of Orkney—to Ireland (where he wrote his first poem), to Norway (where he won a girl in a game of draughts), to Iceland (where his brother was murdered), to Jerusalem (where he "saw the hills where God walked"). Now, stricken by the "black cough" he prepares for his last voyage to death thinking thoughts of the sea:

> I have said to Erling Saltfingers, *Drop my harp*
> *Through a green wave, off Yesnaby,*
> *Next time you row to the lobsters.*

Arnor also figures in 'Viking Testament', a companion poem, in which a Viking divides his estate among his family giving his land to his son Thorstein, his boat to his son Erling (an Eynhallow monk), and a rune by Arnor to his daughter Sigrid.

In 'The Coat', a poem in the ballad metre, Brown adumbrates the garment theme of his novel *Magnus*. Men weave around their bodies a protective persona to shield them from the world. Circumstances, however, strip them of this garment so they are as vulnerable as Christ was when he was stripped before his crucifixion:

> Naked we come and we go.
> Even the Incarnate One
> Shed his seamless splendour
> Under a sackcloth sun.

'Carol' is stitched together with a single rhyme that links the stanzas (bled/dead/red/head/seed/blade/bread) in a consideration of the symbolic ways in which Christ is constantly recrucified (for example in the cutting of the corn).

Death is never far away: a recurring image in Brown's work is the deserted island populated only by the dead. In 'Kirkyard' the corpses become "A silent conquering army". A victim of the army of death is the heroine of 'Sea Orpheus' in which the sea itself makes lyrical poetry as it washes over her drowned body, unable to look back because it

> Had more to do than pity
> A sinking mouth, or heed
> One mortal cornstalk whispering
> A legend of resurrection
> Among the spindrift.

The judicious use of enjambement—so the lines roll into others like waves—suggests the swelling music of the sea.

After these short poems Brown presents a five-part sequence on the ways of kings, 'The Masque of Princes'. 'Sea Jarl' is spoken by Arkol the skald in 1015. A Norwegian king has laid successful seige to a city on the Seine for forty days—during which "The city rotted slowly/Like a spotted corpse in a charnel"—and his men spend seven days in plunder. 'The Lord of the Mirrors' moves on to 1130 Narbonne where a troubador, Bernard, is celebrating the investiture of a new prince by providing earthy answers to romantic questions:

> Beast, what is love?
> Phallus, rut, spasm
>
> Peasant, what is love?
> Plough, furrow, seed
>
> Priest, what is love?
> Prophecy, event, ritual

Bonnie Prince Charlie is the subject of the third poem, 'Prince in the Heather' (supposedly spoken by a Gaelic bard). This is a catalogue of post-Culloden disasters linked by the repeated phrase "Who would have thought. . . ." It is felt that the prince who persuaded the clans to fight betrayed them by leaving the scene of the battle:

> Who would have thought our prince, that hero,
> While we plucked broken steel from the forge of our valour,
> Would take to the screes, a frightened stag?

The sequence ends with a prose-poem, 'King of Kings', a clever variation on the theme of Christ's nativity. The inn-keeper at Bethlehem has turned spy and reports on the drinking and lusting on his premises. Into this squalid atmosphere come "a man and woman from the north" to sleep in the byre; also three wise men (an Egyptian, an Indian, a Chinese). This inn is the unlikely birthplace of Christianity.

After two sets of runes, 'Runes from a Holy Island' (set on Eynhallow, from the Norse *Eyin helga* for holy isle) and 'Runes from the Island of Horses' (set on the Orkney mainland once known by the Norse name of Hrossey, horse island) Brown offers a Yeatsian pastiche. Yeats's 'When You Are Old' begins

> When you are old and grey and full of sleep,
> And nodding by the fire, take down this book . . .

while Brown has

> Some night when you are gray
> And lonely, by muttering flame . . .
> Take up my book. . . .

Both poems are about the withering of beauty, and both are based on a French Renaissance original: Ronsard's celebrated 'Sonnet to Helen' beginning "Quand vous serez bien vielle" (the phrase Brown used for an earlier version of the poem published in *Twelve Poems*). It is, though, the voice of Yeats, not Ronsard, that echoes in Brown's poem which is—being a version of a version of a sixteenth-century poem—inevitably at a remove from reality.

'Tinkers' is, in my opinion, the best of the new poems. In seven quatrains Brown pays a magnificent tribute to these anarchic figures who have haunted his imagination. Though they are ragged they rule the street; though their fiddle has but one string they make marvellous music on it. Their material poverty does not disguise the fact that their presence brings a wild poetry to Hamnavoe:

> Princes, they ruled in our street
> A long shining age,
> While Merran peeped through her curtains
> Like a hawk from a cage.

The last of the new poems is a prose piece, 'The Wedding Guest'. In *Magnus* the Orkney saint meditates on the parable (*Matthew* 22) in which Christ compares heaven to a marriage feast to which a wedding guest must come attired in immaculate garments. In Brown's prose-poem a dead man heads for the Brough of Birsay, the tidal island where Magnus was born and buried. While the monks of Birsay celebrate their faith the sea subsides and the guest's way is clear; his journey ends, with Joycean euphony, as "a dozen doves, clustered, query round the slipway, and enfold him, and out at sea a raven sail, wind laden, westward urgently leans".

43

Winterfold

Winterfold (1976) begins and ends with a Christian sequence, twin testaments to Brown's religious faith. One of the problems of retelling the Story (and implying the Fable) of Christ in our time is that the biblical account is almost contemptibly familiar. Brown's answer to this artistic challenge is to impose a cunning structure on the old old story so that something of the original brilliance shines through. The title sequence, Winterfold, is in five parts of which the first, 'Bethlehem', has an ingenious pattern. There are seven six-line stanzas and in the first of these a line apiece is spoken by, respectively, Angel, Innkeeper, Our Lady, Captain of Herod's Guard, Shepherd, Magus. The order then revolves cyclically, starting with a Magus. This method is ideographic: statements are juxtaposed instead of appearing in sequence. The abrupt shifts from line to line convey something of the confusion surrounding the birth in the byre.

In the second part, 'The Golden Door', the three Magi takes turns to speak, each responding individually to the star of Bethlehem. 'Yule' introduces the "marked tree ... the winter tree" and in part four, 'The Keeper of the Midnight Gate' cynically reacts to the shepherds, the Magi, Mary and Joseph, Herod's captain and the angel:

> I did not think
> Angels stank and had holes in their sleeves.

The sequence closes with a 'Poem for SHELTER' (the campaign for the homeless). Though Christ could rise to glory from "a poor hovel with a star peeking through rafters" such poverty should not be inflicted on mortals, for "the children of time, their rooftrees should be strong".

This powerful sequence is followed, incongruously, by three 'Tea Poems'. Brown begins with an imitation of the simple narrative delicacy of Chinese poetry (at least as a Chinese style has percolated to the West via Waley and Pound): in 'Chinamen' tea is "the water of offered friendship". 'Smugglers' amusingly tells a tale of incompetent Orkneymen: they have come too late and all there is left for them on a Dutch smuggling ship is tea, "women's swill", a poor substitute for the tobacco and silk they expected. The third tea poem is a porcelain painting of Orkneywomen at their 'Afternoon Tea'—Mrs Leask extends a genteel pinkie, Mrs Spence fortifies the tea with whisky, Bella the tea-wife reads fortunes in the dregs.

A collection of Brown's work without some reference to his patron saint Magnus would hardly be the genuine article: 'April the Sixteenth' alludes to the fact that Magnus was martyred on 16 April 1117. The faithful come with all they can muster and the greatest blessing falls on "the poor of the island". After the spare catalogues in 'Fiddlers at the Harvest Home' we are given eight 'Twelfth Century Norse Lyrics' by Magnus's nephew Rognvald Kolson. Earl Rognvald has thirty-two skaldic poems in the *Orkneyinga Saga* and Brown's versions are based on the translations by A. B. Taylor whose edition of the saga has been an inspirational source-book for him. Brown adds a sweet fluency to Taylor's translations. In another translation, 'Deor', Brown turns the Old English alliterative poem (in which the eponymous poet claims that time will triumph over sorrow) into a rhymed poem with a Yeatsian refrain, "That sorrow withered, so may this" (a musical equivalent of the Anglo Saxon "Thaes ofereode, thisses swa maeg"). The whole process whereby poems are transformed, by translation, into original works is considered in 'Seven Translations of a Lost Poem'. Were seven poets to translate the same poem the result would be seven different stylistic results. Thus Brown presents seven different versions of the same events—how a man lost a leg after encountering a prostitute, how he derived small comfort from an irascible poet, how he is unprepared for death.

Apart from the closing sequence and 'The Escape of the Hart' (another look at Bonnie Prince Charlie after Culloden) and 'Eynhallow: Crofter and Monastery' (a dogmatic poem on the twelve monks whose faith preserves them on the little island), the remaining poems plunge us into the sea. A grim humour pervades 'The Desertion of the Women and Seals', a rhymed (*abcbadcd*) poem in which poetic justice is inflicted on the avaricious Howie. He plans to woo reluctant women with money earned by selling sealskin. As any reader of Brown knows, seals are semi-sacred creatures from Orkney folklore and they escape Howie's attentions as easily as the inland lasses have before them. In three harp-songs, 'Vikings', Brown steps back into the past. The first of these, 'Bjorn the Shetlander Sails to Largs 1263', contains a brilliant use of irony. In July 1263 King

45

Hakon of Norway sailed to Scotland with a vast fleet in an attempt to show he was entitled to hold his Scottish possessions including Orkney and Shetland. A combination of storms and Scottish resistance shattered the Norse fleet but the fifteen-year-old narrator of the poem does not know he is sailing to his death:

> Tomorrow with Paul and Sverr my brothers
> I sail for Scotland.
> A thousand sea-borne swords, a golden mask.

The other two harp-songs are less intense: 'The New Skipper' shows Vikings intent on trade rather than raid; 'A Battle in Ulster' recounts the fate of three unfortunate Vikings.

Four elegies make up the sequence 'The Sea'. It is not surprising that an Orkneyman should have such an intimate knowledge of the sea but rare indeed to find a modern poet capable of resuscitating kennings in such a convincing manner as Brown does in 'The Sea':

> The sea is the Great Sweet Mother.
> She is the Swan's Path.
> She is the Whale's Acre.
> She is the Garden of White Roses.
> She is the Keeper of Horses.

The three subsequent elegies in this sequence enumerate various deaths by drowning. Like the element itself the men who extract a living from the sea are shaped by rough winds. One of them, whose trade was herring and shark fishing, was as vicious as the sea and his funeral is described in a poem called 'Unpopular Fisherman'. The world, Brown tells us in eight stanzas, will be a happier place now he is gone:

> Look for no lawless cradles in Quoylay more.
> Wholesome the fights
> With no more gouging, blasphemy, broken bottles
> On Saturday nights.

In 'Sea Widow' Brown picks up the theme of the wailing women or, in this case, one wailing woman. There are four parts: the first,

'Silence', contains the woman's confession of guilt and remorse because she failed to keep her husband from the sea—"I said nothing". In the second part, 'Lost Lovers', she reflects on the husband she might have had—a rich respectable merchant—instead of the man who took her "to a door marked with salt, and with tar and weed". The third and finest part comprises 'What the Fisherman Said'. It is a beautiful lyric full of promises (the man is determined to renounce smoking and drinking) and good intentions:

> I will build you a house with my hands,
> A stored cupboard,
> Undying hearth-flames, a door open to friend and stranger.

However, we find in the final part—'Wedding Ring'—that the promises were not kept, the good intentions were not fulfilled. There were only four perfect moments,

> Four circles of grace.
> The rest were pub-stoked lurchings, blood on his face.

The story this short sequence tells is sad and bitter; the man is sacrificed to the sea and leaves behind a broken widow and a fatherless child.

Winterfold closes with 'Stations of the Cross', a ten-part sequence in which some key features of Brown's poetry coalesce. There is the fondness for numerical order (each poem has fourteen sections corresponding to the fourteen stations of Christ's Passion); there is the love of counterpoint (each poem embodies a contrast with the life of Christ); there is the mixture of the everyday and the eternal (the Story of a man, the Fable of mankind); there is the multiple viewpoint (so the same central situation is seen from various angles). The first poem, 'From Stone to Thorn', is in fact the lyric, 'Stations of the Cross', from *Fishermen with Ploughs*; it now gives the overall title to the sequence. In an introductory note to *Winterfold*, Brown apologises for the appearance of this lyric "yet again". No need to apologise—most readers would welcome it. It becomes the starting point for the sequence and the subsequent poems are modelled on it.

The second part, 'Pilate', speaks with an indifferent voice. Whereas in 'From Stone to Thorn', Christ's First Fall became the

47

crofter's hard amorous embrace of the earth ("To drudge in furrows
till you drop/Is to be born") Pilate looks at the same event in a very
different way:

> I was told later he bent a knee
> Between the cupid and the rose bush.
> The gardener told me that later, laughing.

'The Lesser Mysteries of Art', the third part, is an interesting artistic
credo: we are told that the symbol "outlasts roses,/statues,/even the
grief of women". As if to demonstrate the truth of this assertion
Brown uses a symbol of death in 'Hawk' where the bird is at the
mercy of its Godlike master; and in 'Potter and Jar', a perfectly
turned wine jar becomes Christ's body when the potter, Adam, stores
it in the sepulchre of his cellar.

The analogies multiply. In 'The Stone Cross', Christ's Passion is
implicit in a Viking raid on an Irish monastery, while in 'Sea
Village' Christ becomes an Orkney fisherman, Ollie Manson,
condemned for his refusal to bow to the local laird. Ollie's Third Fall
is attributed to his passion for radical politics:

> Socialist books, that was the start of it.
> I blame the dominie.
> Paine and Blatchford, they'll bring him down.

In a series of striking images the eighth-part, 'Creator', invokes the
spirit of Christ ("He is the Winter Tree dragged by a peasant").
'Kingdom of Dust' has a particularly beautiful image when
Veronica wiping the face of Christ becomes a man seeking comfort in
the eyes of a weeping woman: "He put the red mud of his face in a
crumpled mirror". The sequence ends with 'Carpenter' in which a
fallen tree can become either a gallows or a cradle for Mary's child.
The images have been given a life of their own.

All Brown's poems have a distinctive voice though it is sometimes
formal (as in 'Stations of the Cross') and sometimes direct and
natural ('Sea Widow'). Although he has immersed himself in
literature and learned from religious poets like Herbert and Hopkins
and modern poets like Yeats and Eliot, Brown adheres above all to

the strong rhythms of the oral tradition—as preserved in the ballads and the sagas. Whatever the idiom, he tries to speak for a whole people and he always expresses himself eloquently in a clear Orkney accent. It is a way of saying extraordinary things in an apparently ordinary way.

3   Storyteller

George Mackay Brown's greatest achievement, in my opinion, is to be found in his ability as a storyteller. It is a gift, a remarkable ability, and he is unique in his matter and manner (though he has learned from the writing of Thomas Mann, E. M. Forster, Jorge Luis Borges). In fellow Orkneyman, Eric Linklater, he had a modern precedent for the use of Orkney material as a basis for fiction but Brown's work is unlike Linklater's in that it goes beyond the exigencies of a strict narrative to concentrate on the essential spirituality of a given situation. This is not to say that Brown wants to communicate only an other-worldly beauty; on the contrary many of his stories deal with the brutal necessity of a hard working life. There is much melancholy in his work, as much tribulation as there is triumph. Yet the symbolic framework within which Brown works— where the symbol adds an enduring shine to the activities of the folk—adds a deep formal perspective to the scenes that hold his attention. He imposes a religious and artistic vision on his narrative so that it is shaped for survival.

He writes in short sentences whose finality has an autonomous feel. The deliberate step-by-step construction of the tale, within a solid structural matrix, conveys a classical feeling of inevitability. The silences matter, too, for there is a stanzaic pause between paragraphs and the stories are usually split into sections by a trinity of asterisks.

A Calendar of Love

His first collection of stories, *A Calendar of Love*, appeared in February 1967 when the author was forty-five and best-known for his two collections of poetry, *Loaves and Fishes* and *The Year of the Whale*. It was an immensely important moment for Brown in demonstrating that his prose was an even sharper instrument than his verse. Since that first book of stories Brown has gone on to become Scotland's finest living writer of imaginative prose and it is interesting to observe that all the characteristic features are already there, in that first collection. The form of the stories is determined by numbers and counterpoint while the content is entirely derived from Orkney's past and present—the stories range in time from 1150 AD (when Norsemen violated Maes Howe prior to joining Earl Rognvald's pilgrimage to Jerusalem) to the 1960s. Brown's stories are not concerned with the spinning out of a plot so much as exploring the richest aspects of a given situation. To use Edwin Muir's phraseology, the Story is constantly moving towards Fable.

The title story is an example of Brown's use of the symbol to give a miraculous side to a story. For on the face of it the piece is a tough slice of parochial life told with restraint and impersonality. As well as the habit of breaking his stories up into stanza and section, an added episodic quality is apparent in the title-story by the monthly divisions of the year. The fascination with numbers is repeated in the existence of three principal characters, a trinity. The woman, Jean Scarth, is the static centre round which revolve the other two protagonists: Peter, the fisherman, a bible-puncher; and Thorfinn Vik, a crofter who is known to hit the bottle.

It is 1962 and Jean Scarth is trying to run the Ingsevay Inn after the death of her father. She is pursued by Peter and Thorfinn and while she respects the fisherman's temperance she is moved by the crofter's passionate nature. In March—the agricultural seedtime— both men possess her: Thorfinn in his green van (the wanderer), Peter in her home (the settler). There has been a death so there must be a birth—unless this happens in Brown's stories there is an ominous impression of the imminent death of a community. Yet Jean Scarth has to cope with the repressive presbyterian spirit of condemnation. She becomes ashamed of the child she is carrying. She keeps herself to herself with her "precious shameful burden" (p. 27).

The real hero of the story is a symbol. In November, right on cue, falls winter's first snowflake whose natural purity has supernatural overtones. On Peter, mentally crippled by religious fanaticism, the snowflake falls like forgiveness. On Thorfinn, twisted with violence, it falls like a peace-offering. On Jean it falls like a blessing, like a heavenly seed, and as it falls (p. 33)

> suddenly everything was in its place. The tinkers would move for ever through the hills. Men would plough their fields.

> Men would bait their lines. . . . And forever the world would
> be full of youth and beauty, birth and death, labouring and
> suffering.

Against this elemental background Jean welcomes the child as a
creature capable of renewing her world. What Brown has done is to
reinvest with poetic significance an event that people have come to
take for granted.

After 'A Calendar of Love' comes 'Five Green Waves'—the
numerical title indicating the divisions of the story. Here the
narrative is in the first person, comprising the recollections of a
primary schoolboy who, during the story, is transformed by five
experiences that wash over him. First, a wave of disapproval from his
schoolteacher begins his voyage home to report his failure (to learn
the theorum of Pythagoras) to his father. Stopping en route at an old
sailor's house he is given "a dark seething wave" (p. 44) of ale which,
combined with the impact of a lurid ballad, makes him vomit. The
third wave is the feeling that comes over him when, emerging naked
from the sea near the kirkyard, he meets Sarah—a tinker's daughter.
She roughs him up in response to an amorous suggestion then, as
"She waved and shouted" (p. 51), she tempts him. The fourth wave
is a contemplation of the "slow tide that sets towards eternity" (p.
52) prompted by a gravestone to an unknown foreign sailor.

Like many of his stories, 'Five Green Waves' consists of an odyssey
and when the voyager, the child-narrator, reaches home he listens to
his father's sound advice about setting course for a decent profession.
These intimations of respectability are interrupted by the passing of
the tinkers' cart, tinkers being in Brown's iconography the ragged
personifications of anarchic freedom. Sarah, the tinker's daughter,
has a bunch of wild lupins in her arms and she throws them at the boy
so that, for the fifth and final wave, "A wave of purple blossom rose in
front of the moon and showered over me" (p. 60). This sudden shock
of beautiful mockery contains enough enchantment to offer an
uncertain alternative to getting-on in the world. The boy has been
through a journey with significant stops (or stations if we want to
stress the religious parallel). He is transformed by the five waves of
experience from a schoolboy to a youngster with thoughts about life
and love and death. The first sentence in the story, "Time was lines

and circles and squares" (p. 41), is thus reversed in the last sentence of the story, "Time was skulls and butterflies and guitars" (p. 60). The child has learned more on his voyage home from school than he did in the arid atmosphere of the geometry lesson.

The use of counterpoint, so crucial to Brown's approach, is seen to advantage in the third story, another numerical title 'The Three Islands'. Counterpoint is, of course, the juxtaposition of contrasts. In this story the present is counterpointed against the past. Each island in the story gets a section to itself; within each section the pressures of the present are set against the permanence of the past. The islands are Eynhallow (Norse *Eyin helga*, the holy island), site of a monastery; Gairsay, site of the *Langi Skali* (long hall) of the Viking adventurer Sweyn Asleifson, a prominent figure in the *Orkneyinga Saga*; and Egilsay, where on 16 April 1117 Earl Magnus was slain on the orders of his cousin, Earl Hakon.

Brown links the three islands by the convention of a voyage, a fishing trip involving three men (one of whom narrates the story). As the men are taken up in their task of hauling lobster creels they are unaware of the rich past of the islands they pass. So Brown provides the twelfth-century presence. In Eynhallow, a scribe writes up the tale of Everyman while on Gairsay, Sweyn Asleifson embarks on a pre-harvest raid and returns minus three men (again, the number three). On Egilsay it is Easter Monday, the morning of Magnus's martyrdom and an old priest (who will reappear in the novel *Magnus*) intent on the Mass has his thoughts disturbed by the presence of Magnus inside the church and his followers outside. Brown is suggesting that the busy fishermen ignore this rich past at their peril; without it their lives are reduced to a series of direction-less voyages.

As an extension of his use of counterpoint Brown is careful to include in each of his collections a number of brief pieces appreciably less intense than the main items. These do not explore themes in the symbolic manner of the big stories but are content to expand an anecdote. In *A Calendar of Love* there are five anecdotal interludes, four of them coming immediately after the richness of 'The Three Islands'. 'The Seller of Silk Shirts' is narrated by Johnny, a Sikh pedlar, who will later turn up in *Greenvoe*; 'The Wheel' is a short account of a man driven to cyclical distraction since the drowning of his closest friend; 'The Troubling of the Water' is a cautionary tale about home-made whisky; and 'The Ferryman' consists of various ongoings between the shores of Hoy and the Mainland. An even finer short piece, 'Tam', comes after a rather mechanical Play for Voices—'The Storm Watchers'—in which seven women wait for the bodies of their men to be brought ashore. Tam is a young Orkneyman who, on his way to catch a boat going to Hudson's Bay or the Davis Straits, stops at a cousin's house and sows his seed in the three daughters of the house. After his departure "three bonny bairns, born within a week of each other, played on the steps of the close where Jock the shoemaker lived" (p. 103). Tam is survived by his seed.

With 'Witch' we are on another level and Brown simulates the sights and sounds of the sixteenth century. It is a tale of the most appalling and arbitrary inhumanity. Having endured the barbarities of Earl Robert Stewart (a half-brother to Mary Queen of Scots), Orkney is now in the cruel grip of Earl Patrick Stewart who simply took over where his father left off. Earl Patrick, who was eventually executed in Edinburgh in 1615, is now remembered for commissioning the Earl's Palace in Kirkwall, a fine piece of Renaissance architecture. Brown uses Earl Patrick as a symbol of cultured indifference to suffering (in this he resembles the narrator of Browning's poem 'My Last Duchess') and as such his shadow hangs oppressively over 'Witch' and, later, a key section of the title-story of *Hawkfall*. The magnificent palace in Kirkwall is the setting for the totally unjust witch-trial.

The story concerns one Marian Isbister who is charged with witchcraft after rebuffing the amorous advances of Earl Patrick's factor Stephen Buttquoy. In other words, it is a put-up job— something easily arranged in an authoritarian society. Marian is taken to Kirkwall, cruelly probed with a needle, taken through the formality of a trial (during which some bear false witness against her) and condemned. To prepare her for burning her head is shaved and her fingernails and toe-nails are extracted; on the way to Gallowsha "she hobbled . . . with her fingers like a tangle of red roots at the end of her long white arms, and her head like an egg" (p. 121). After all this she is shown kindness by, of all people, the executioner, Piers, who strangles her before the fire is lit. The local people have a great celebration (Earl Patrick having decreed a public holiday) and, as the story ends, we are transported to Edinburgh where James VI of

Scotland (and future James I of England) initiates an official inquiry into the atrocities of his cousin Earl Patrick Stewart.

For all his emphasis on the typicality of the individual and his fondness for communal life, Brown is well aware of what can happen when individuals lose their personal heads to become part of the tidal wave of irrationality that can engulf a small community. Like the witch in *A Spell for Green Corn*, Marian Isbister is a convenient scapegoat. At one time the burning of witches was all too common in Orkney. Brown's tale of the murder of innocence is calculated to arouse indignation in the modern reader and yet, for all its depiction of superstition and cruelty, 'Witch' is technically one of the most subdued of Brown's stories, a model of impersonality which lets the facts speak for themselves and leaves the reader to form his own opinion of what happened. The narrator is a sixteenth-century clerk simply recording what he has seen, and Brown is wonderfully adept at imitating the style of archaic prose. There is a minimum of description and a maximum of dialogue making the piece more of a short play than a short story. This oblique approach has the advantage of making the account terribly believable. Were it not for its inclusion in a modern collection of stories the reader might well believe that he was perusing an authentic sixteenth-century document.

We remain in the sixteenth century for the next tale, 'Master Halcrow, Priest'. The story is told by the eponymous priest, a man approaching seventy who "fishes and drinks too much" (p. 125). It is 1561 and Knox has officially established the Reformation in Scotland. All this is news to Father Halcrow as he is ejected from his church, St Peter's; replaced by a young presbyterian minister; and denounced by a former priest Magnus Anderson. As this Anderson's illicit liaison with a huge mountain of a woman was a cause of great mirth in the parish, the angry Father Halcrow flings an accusation of lust in the face of Anderson. Having taken such a bitter leave of the Protestants, Father Halcrow wanders on the beach and contemplates the religious symbolism of the stones (p. 131): "did not the very name Peter mean stone, permanence, unassailability?" Suddenly he remembers he has left the pyx in the church, and returns to find St Peter's desecrated, the statues of Our Lady and St Peter and St Magnus cast down iconoclastically. But Magnus Anderson has hidden the pyx and clandestinely passes it to Father

Halcrow with a promise that he will come to perform the last rites on the old man. Catholicism has gone underground. It is not the end of Father Halcrow for his voice is heard again in one of Brown's greatest stories, 'A Treading of Grapes' in *A Time to Keep*.

The last three stories in *A Calendar of Love* dwell on loss. 'The Ballad of the Rose Bush' is concerned with the fate of Margaret, a dumb girl. When her brothers find her, bleeding and dishevelled, at a well they automatically assume that the guilty party is Mick the tinker, composer of a new reel, 'The Rose Bush'. The family pride is satisfied when Mick is hanged at Gallowsha three days before Christmas. Those who know the Scottish traditional ballads will also know that a classic resolution of any tale of true love is the rose-and-briar ending whereby his grave sprouts a rose-bush and hers a briar. And, yes, Margaret dies embroidering a briar with a red rose in the heart of it; and, yes, a rose bush grows out of Mick's grave. On this poetic logic, then, Margaret and Mick were true lovers and one Clod the shepherd is the culprit. The tale uses a limpid prose to convey the inevitability and impersonality of the traditional ballad.

'Stone Poems' occurs inside the chambered cairn of Maes Howe. It is a historical fact that, prior to joining Earl Rognvald's crusade in 1150, Norsemen entered Maes Howe and left behind runic inscriptions. Letting his imagination work on this, Brown settles for seven poets (the obligatory seven) to make a significant number of invaders in the petrified womb. We go through the seven inscriptions (actually one of the invaders, an illiterate, draws a dragon instead of a rune—an unconvincing detail this, as the Maes Howe dragon is no amateur piece of graffiti but the work of a considerable artist). The final inscription is the most interesting: "In the North-West is a great treasure hidden". Brown makes this no secular treasure but "the bones of the blessed Magnus that lie in the Birsay kirk ten miles north-west from this place" (p. 146).

Last of all is 'The Story of Jorkel Hayforks'. Seven men set out from Norway to Hoy so that their leader, Jorkel, can settle an account with the father of his sister's bastard. At each stage of their voyage a man is lost—one seduced by a woman, one falling from a cliff, one dying at sea, one becoming a monk, one stung to death by bees—until only Jorkel and Valt reach Hoy. There Jorkel slays his sister's seducer; in the ensuing battle Valt is killed and Jorkel is lacerated with hayforks (hence his name). He settles in Hoy and a long intimacy with the good earth mellows him so that the story ends as he visits his shipmate-become-monk to ask for a mass for himself and for his sister's seducer.

A Calendar of Love is a fine collection of stories that display a unity as a result of the indigenous context. Brown had shown how many variations he could spin round the history and the legends of the Orkneys. He had shown, too, in 'Witch' a command of the prose style of another era. Henceforth the manner and method would remain the same; the approach does not alter, basically, but gets more and more linguistically suggestive.

A Time to Keep

A Time to Keep (1969) has a biblical title (*Ecclesiastes* 3); a religious faith underpins the events enacted in the book. This is not a question of dogma but a quiet certainty of the worth of each individual no matter how economically afflicted, no matter how unworthy in the eyes of others. It is expressed in the third sermon of that superb story 'A Treading of Grapes' (p. 74):

> each one of you has in his keeping an immortal soul, a rich jewel indeed, more precious than all the world beside.

It is this that draws the author to such low-lifers as Celia, and to such human wrecks as Captain Stevens (in 'The Eye of the Hurricane'). For Brown makes sure the reader sees through the superficial appearance of Celia, the alcoholic, and notices the spiritual despair; and he shows that the wreck that is Captain Stevens was ruined on a beautiful love and the tragic loss of that love.

Of the dozen stories in *A Time to Keep* four—'Celia', 'A Time to Keep', 'A Treading of Grapes', 'The Eye of the Hurricane'—are major achievements, while the remaining stories range from the accomplished to the excellent. There is no hint of failure in the writing itself, yet the notion of failure—of defeat—is what the book is, thematically, all about. *A Time to Keep* is the most firmly unromantic of Brown's books; the one where his imagination is most solidly rooted in the reality of actual life. The vivid characters in the stories are shaped by a grinding economic poverty that crushes them; that makes them despair of attaining anything but a corresponding

57

spiritual poverty. Still, there is an imaginatively fulfilling world beyond the closes of Hamnavoe and the open cruelty of the sea and Brown introduces it as a highlight to emphasise the surrounding shadows of distress.

For the eponymous anti-heroine of 'Celia' this imaginative world—the kingdom of her dreams—has to be alcoholically induced. Sitting drinking in the literal and metaphorical gloom of her room in a house on a fishermen's pier, she tells a Presbyterian minister (p. 21):

> This kingdom I've had a glimpse of, though—what about that? ... Why do we have to struggle towards it through fogs of drink? What's the good of all this mystery? The vision should be like a loaf or a fish, simple and real, something given to nourish the whole world.

In the presbyterian tradition drink is something evil taken by evil people to sustain their evil natures; so it is not surprising that Celia's confession falls on deaf ears. For, as she explains, she is not merely an alcoholic, she is a woman who casually sells her body in exchange for drink. So the drink that brings her release from the everyday drudgery is obtained in a sordid way that, inevitably, increases the guilt-edged insecurity of her hangovers.

Celia has two principal men in her life: Thomas Linklater her stepfather, a shoemaker; and Ronald Leask, a crofter. Leask's declarations of love for Celia are frequently thrown back, ferociously, in his face. As a gesture, to assuage his frustration and to defend Celia's honour, he gets obsessively drunk and assaults a Norwegian sailor who is known to visit Celia. This provokes a vicious pub brawl and while the participants are being locked away Celia tells her stepfather she will marry Ronald—more to please a dying man than because of her feelings. She looks out into the harbour and the sun comes over the Orphir hills to offer Celia the solace of a new day.

Brown's triumph here is the way he depicts Celia—ostensibly a drunken tart—as a human being of worth. He does this with a totally convincing act of empathy when he lets the character speak for herself. Her confession to the minister is not the maudlin self-pity of the habitual drunk but a believable statement made by a hypersensitive person (p. 15):

I drink because I'm frightened. I'm so desperately involved with all the weak things, lonely things, suffering things I see about me. I can't bear the pity I feel for them.

Having established this area of Celia's personality Brown surrounds her with insensitivity: the men who buy her with a bottle of whisky, the poverty of her childhood. Using his own artistic gifts he bestows on this lovely, abused-by-love, conventionally unloveable creature the euphony and vowel-music of his prose so that her world is cleansed by natural images. Note how the liquidity of the "l" sounds suggest the promise of peace (p. 37):

> The first seagulls were screaming along the street, scavenging in the bins. She breathed the clean air of early morning. . . . The sun had not yet risen, but light was assembling in broken colours over the Orphir hills. The first blackbird in the fuchsia bush under the watchmaker's wall faltered into song and then was silent again. . . . It would be a beautiful morning.

The title story of *A Time to Keep* is set in Rackwick on Hoy, one of Brown's favourite parts of Orkney. It is told in the first person of Bill, a crofter-fisherman, who is determined to go his own way in the valley and avoid the presbyterian negativity of his neighbours. He is proud of being a freethinker and is set for a clean independent start with a new wife Ingi, a new house, a new plough, a new boat, and a new field dug at the side of the house. He is conscious of his poverty— "We're poor people. Remember that" (p. 42), he tells his wife—but aware too that the land and the sea are there to sustain life (p. 50):

> A green offering hand, our valley, corn-giver, fire-giver, water-giver, keeper of men and beasts. The other hand that fed us was this blue hand of the sea, which was treacherous, which had claws to it, which took more than ever it gave.

Bill is not interested in being a part of the community—apart from the community that gathers nightly in the ale-house—and he becomes an isolated figure in the valley. He is also at odds with Ingi's father—a merchant, kirk elder, Justice of the Peace, chairman of the district council—who embodies presbyterian respectability. Bill has no faith in the church but great faith in the soil and the sea and he watches his oatfield move "like a great slow green wave all summer" (p. 54), waiting for a golden harvest. As is usual in Brown's work the whole ritual of birth is implied: just as the seed has been planted in the ploughed earth to ripen, so Bill's seed has been planted in Ingi.

Disaster, however, overwhelms Bill in a double tragedy that is presented contrapuntally. First we see the cornfield ruined by rain, "all squashed and tangled" (p. 54); then we see Ingi ruined in childbirth, "Her damp hair sprawled all over the pillow" (p. 57). Ingi is dead, "long and pale as a quenched candle" (p. 58). With his stoical nature Bill endures her death and the dreadful ritualistic wailing of the women. He feels fated to return to fish in the sea. It is a desolate tale made bearable by the beauty of the descriptions and the stark images of men scything the fields and cooling their throats with ale. It is a portrait of a community in decline, chilled by a cold religion. By the 1950s Rackwick had died as a community and the story of its communal birth, decline and fall is recounted in Brown's poem-sequence *Fishermen with Ploughs*. 'A Time to Keep' preserves, in the amber of imaginative prose, what life must have been like in Rackwick for one man: a cycle of toil and tragedy.

On purely stylistic grounds 'A Treading of Grapes' is the finest piece in the book. It combines counterpoint with the multiple viewpoint to give three distinct ways of looking at the same event. This event is a biblical one, the marriage in Cana (*John* 2) where Christ turned water into wine. Brown offers three sermons on the subject, supposedly preached through the ages by three different incumbents of St Peter's Church, Orkney. The verisimilitude and clever introduction make it difficult to realise that this is not a documentary history but a purely fictional recreation. The three styles employed might be called the flatly modern, the thunderously Knoxian and the richly ritual. As a Catholic, of course, Brown is most attracted to the third style.

However he begins with the recreation of a typical contemporary Church of Scotland sermon, full of folksy humour and commonsensical observations. In this there was no miracle, but Christ, like a canny Scot, made sure extra supplies of wine were laid in. The second sermon is supposed to have been delivered by Dr Thomas Fortheringhame in August 1788. This Church of Scotland man— obviously of the Auld Licht faction of extreme Calvinists—has more fire in his belly than his twentieth-century counterpart and he breathes his hellfire into the Godfearing faces of his congregation. The negativity of Knoxism is revealed by the way the Rev Fortheringhame uses the biblical text as a moral stick with which to beat his parishioners: because the Lord had wine does not give "divine permission to you to make drunken beasts of yourselves at every wedding" (p. 67). Relying on scatological imagery he reminds them of a local wedding where "all the guests lay at the ale-kirn like piglets about the teats of a sow till morning" (p. 67) and counsels them to have discretion in their eating habits and not "hog down your brose like swine in a sty or like cuddies at a trough" (p. 69). At the end of his moralistic sermon the minister incidentally demands a share of some stolen cargo, a keg of best brandy. Thus Brown neatly illustrates the hypocrisy of a Church of Scotland minister. Fortheringhame is a bit of a caricature, drawn in part from Burns's great ecclesiastical satires.

The final sermon, the story suggests, was preached by Father John Halcrow in 1548 (and we remember this priest from 'Master Halcrow, Priest' in *A Calendar of Love*). Expertly simulating sixteenth-century prose, Brown makes the priest's sermon a beautifully sonorous passage of writing, rich in imagery and compassion, a marvellous piece of eloquence indicating that the priest was simultaneously in touch with God above and the poor folk below. He dwells on the miraculous nature of Christ's act and involves the congregation in the miracle by emphasising that they figure prominently in Christ's divinity. Economically they may be destitute but spiritually they are rich, each having "an immortal soul, a rich jewel indeed, more precious than all the world beside" (p. 74). And as Brown leaves us with the memory of that magnificent sermon he sets the whole sequence in the Orkney landscape with a dazzling piece of alliterative euphony and onomatopoetic music (pp. 75–6):

> The sea shattered and shattered on the beach.
> The wind from the sea soughed under the eaves of the Kirk, and among tombstones with texts and names newly chiselled on them, and those with withered half-obliterated

61

lettering, and those that have lost their meanings and secrets to very ancient rain.

After the majesty of that prose comes 'Icarus', the most whimsical item in the book, an anecdote about an old man who prophesies the end of the world then crashes painfully to earth in an attempt to escape from the doomed planet. 'The Story Teller' contains three tales and the first two are, like 'Icarus', anecdotal. In the Hamnavoe Bar the old storyteller offers tales of 'The Two Women', 'The Fishing Boat' and 'The Fiddler'. The third of these introduces the symbolic note for the first time in the collection. A gifted Rackwick fiddler, Samuel Smith, makes magical curative music. At a big pre-Martinmas concert in Hoy school, however, the folk have grown tired of Samuel's fiddling as they prefer the novelty offered by popular songs played on an accordion by Finlay Oman, a pen-pusher, a "Poor-Boy-who-had-Got-On" (p. 96). At the party the fiddle is smashed, an act of destruction that will break the spell on the island. For the fiddle, in Brown's work, is a symbol of folk art; a sacred instrument on which local men make music in tune with the elements. In a later story in *A Time to Keep*, 'The Bright Spade', there is the spectacle of a fiddle which "once a sweet brimming shell, hung at Jacob's door like a shrivelled chrysalis" (p. 133); in *An Orkney Tapestry* a part of Rackwick dies when "A gramophone with a horn came to the valley, and the fiddle hung at the wall like a dry chrysalis" (p. 50). *A Spell for Green Corn* is a study of the folk art of the fiddle. When Samuel Smith's fiddle, then, is broken into "a hundred bits of varnished wood and a tangle of wires" (p. 99) the old man himself dies.

If the hero of that story is the fiddle, then the villain is not so much Finlay Oman as Finlay Oman's accordion. In Brown's work, novelty is always something to be wary of because it is an ally of Progress and therefore potentially destructive to the community. Finlay's accordion is "huge labouring lung and clicking teeth" (p. 97), a modernist monster. In 'The Wireless Set' the villain is, as the title shows, the radio. Howie Eunson—son of Hugh and Betsy—brings, in 1939, the first radio ever seen in his valley. When war breaks out Howie is killed after his minesweeper is torpedoed. In his father's mind the arrival of the radio is to blame because it coincided with the catastrophe: he smashes the wireless set to pieces. To the slickly modern mind such a causal connexion between an artefact and a human tragedy is meaningless, but Brown succeeds so well in getting inside the primitive mind that we can understand this symbolic act of destruction. The overall impression given is that folk like old Hugh in 'The Wireless Set'—or Bill in 'A Time to Keep'—have had to develop a stoicism that appears insensitive to outsiders. Brown's prose cuts through the stoical surface so that we see the grief behind the mask.

'The Wireless Set' is followed by two whaling stories. The first, 'The Five of Spades', tells of Check Hara, a nineteenth-century Orkneyman whose compulsive gambling separates him from his Clara Moar. He is jailed in Kirkwall; escapes on a ship bound for Nova Scotia; is flogged and put ashore in Newfoundland; and becomes a legendary whaler. Back home he is the subject of a heroic ballad and Clara, patiently expecting her third child, waits in vain for him. At the end of the story we see the reality behind the ballad. A "gnarled insignificant man and an Indian woman and four half-breed children" (p. 113) arrive in Hamnavoe from a Hudson's Bay vessel and slowly slip into obscurity.

Part of Brown's fascination with voyages no doubt comes from familiarity with Login's Well, at the south end of Stromness. The well was sealed up in 1931 but an inscription tells that "there watered here the Hudson Bay Coy's ships 1670–1891". Walking past that well must often have provided Brown's imagination with imaginary voyages. He told me that a "favourite dodge" of his "is to have somebody go from one place to another; in between there are five stopping places + start + finish (eg 'The Whaler's Return')." In 'The Whaler's Return' a gentle man, Flaws, makes his way to Birsay though there are thirty-four ale houses in Hamnavoe and sixteen on the road between Hamnavoe and Birsay. The highlight of his boozy odyssey is seeing a tinkers' wedding. Flaws is one of the most fortunate individuals in the book because he reaches his Penelope (Peterina) and settles down to be contentedly poor ever after. Amusingly, we might note that the whalers can catch great whales but are easily tamed by little women.

After the two whaling stories there is an interlude—'The Bright Spade', a portrait of an overworked gravedigger—then two contrasted Viking stories. 'Tartan' opens splendidly, full of menace. Four Vikings make a raid on Caithness (this, incidentally, is the only

63

story that is not set in Orkney) and one of them, the drunken Kol, utters murderous threats. However, the low cunning of the locals sends them home with only a booty of tartan; Kol ends up in a ditch, his throat cut. There is a comical feeling to 'Tartan'; the other Viking tale, 'A Carrier of Stones', tells a different tale with a religious point to it. A Viking tough, Rolf, is assiduously courted by Orcadians who want use his brute force to bludgeon their enemies. Rolf refuses all offers. At one stage he is challenged to a fight by a Shetlander, Burn, and the ensuing encounter brings forth a splendidly hyperbolic image from Brown. As Rolf grips the Shetlander's hand "Driblets of blood began to well from the burst points of his fingers" (p. 151). Another rich image—or rather a series of linked images— occurs in a description of a woman presented as a temptation to Rolf (pp. 145–6):

> *Her womb is awake. Her body is like a banked-up forge waiting for the thrust of love, the roaring bellows, masses of flame. . . . Her body is like a swept barn in the days before harvest. . . . Her body is like a cupboard, empty and waiting.*

Despite all the temptations of the flesh Rolf, the Viking, ends up a member of the monastery in Birsay.

It is, however, the last story of the book, 'The Eye of the Hurricane', that matches the quality of the first three: the stories in between make a valley between the peaks of, on the one side, 'Celia', 'A Time to Keep', 'A Treading of Grapes'; and, on the other, 'The Eye of the Hurricane'. The story begins as if it were a light-hearted self-portrait of the author. Like Brown, Barclay the narrator works "between breakfast and lunch time" (p. 156)—at a novel— and likes to walk in the afternoons. Like Brown, he is a Catholic writer who wants to enrich the present with the Norse past (his novel is about the holy voyage of Earl Rognvald Kolson). And at one point we find Barclay reading "Alain-Fournier's *Le Grand Meaulnes*, an exquisite rural idyll" (p. 166), while Edwin Muir, writing to Brown from Newbattle on 13 May 1953, advised him to read "Fournier's *Le Grand Meaulnes*, an interesting book which I think would be completely in your world".*

* Ed. P. H. Butter, *Selected Letters of Edwin Muir*, London (The Hogarth Press) 1974, p. 166.

Two distractions disturb Barclay. As he has rented a flat in Captain Stevens's house on Brinkie's Brae, Stromness, he is asked to fetch-and-carry regular supplies of rum to the old captain. The captain's salvationist cleaning girl, Miriam, forbids him to do this as she explains that another ferocious drinking bout could kill the captain. In his novelistic reveries Barclay becomes Rognvald while Miriam becomes the French widow Ermengarde courted by Rognvald in Narbonne. Out of this material Brown weaves a meditation on love, for Barclay discovers on a local tombstone that Captain Stevens's wife Elizabeth died in giving birth to a dead child. While Barclay dreams of possessing Miriam he wakes to find himself ashamed at the extent of his "lascivious imagination" (p. 177).

The climax of this splendid story—in which reality and myth combine in a welter of images—occurs when a drunken Captain Stevens is visited by two old shipmates. He is convinced he is back on ship, trying to steer the crew "through the shining eye of the hurricane" (p. 175). In describing this stormy scene Brown manages to transfer the salt and spray of the sea into the captain's bedroom. For the storm is inside the captain and in this scene it passes out of him and he drops dead. Barclay is full of pity for the dead man and bewildered at the intensity of love (p. 181):

> I know, though I cannot celebrate it, that all these loves are caught up in their true order, and simplified, and reconciled, in the wheel of being whose centre is Incarnation; they move about it forever like the quiet stars.

So *A Time to Keep* ends as it began, by seeing the spiritual energy that activates the sort of human beings the professionally pious despise. Women like Celia and men like Captain Stevens—both hopelessly dependent on alcohol for day-to-day survival—are presented with a genuine artistic depth. We see them as others see them; then as the author sees them; then as they see themselves. After all the torment and despair and bleakness in the book the final impression is one of hope. As a Catholic, Brown believes each individual has an immortal soul; were his stories only to assert this belief then they would only appeal to fellow Catholics. In fact there is nothing dogmatic about the writing and little is taken for granted: each insight is carved out of the material before us.

Hawkfall

In 'The Eye of the Hurricane' Brown used the word "hawkfall" as a kenning for death, for he suggests that Rognvald Kolson's pilgrimage to Jerusalem was undertaken "to delete from history the Viking hawkfall" (p. 167). Given his poet's precision with words, then, it is obvious that the title of Brown's third collection. *Hawkfall* (1974), is meant to stand as a guide to the contents. And indeed *Hawkfall* is a series of variations on the theme of death and destruction, an Orkney book of the dead. There is always the hint of the possibility of renewal and rebirth but the collection makes the reader very much aware of the dead generations cast, like a long shadow, behind the figure of each living individual. There are eleven stories and only two ('The Fight at Greenay', a slight piece about an epic pub brawl; and 'The Burning Harp', an eightieth-birthday tribute to the novelist Neil Gunn) deviate from this theme.

The title story of *Hawkfall* is a meditation, in five parts, on the way history survives in the unmistakeable features of one family on the Orkney mainland. In its timespan and narrative subtlety—which requires an act of imaginative empathy on the part of the reader—it is one of the author's greatest stories. It shows how Brown is capable of suggesting an entire history of Orkney in one tale. Historians hostile to the personalised approach to their subject have advocated a broad thematic methodology and dismissed the individualistic approach as a search for "Cleopatra's nose": Brown's story 'Hawkfall' puts a humble flattened Orkney nose firmly to the forefront of his historical narrative.

The story opens, majestically, in Orkney's Bronze Age. A priest-king has died and is being taken from the Temple of the Sun (the Ring of Brodgar) between the lochs of Harray and Stenness to the House of the Dead (Maes Howe). Apart from the use of the prehistoric monoliths and the megalithic tomb, the opening has another ritual element associated with Brown: the wailing women who follow the body of the priest-king. Ritual life has to go on and a new priest-king is consecrated in the Ring of Brodgar. Meanwhile, in the village of Skarabrae, a fisherman "with a curiously flattened nose" (p. 14) is indifferent to the death of the king. He has his own life to live. This fisherman is to be reborn through his descendents as the story progresses.

We move to the eleventh century for the second section of the story. Thorfinn Sigurdson, the most powerful of the Earls of Orkney, has reached the end of his days in his Hall on the Brough of Birsay, a tidal island often cited in Brown's poems and stories. Absorbed in his past sins he has little time for the boy-servant who makes fires in the Hall. The reader, however, instantly recognises the boy as part of the lineage of the Skarabrae fisherman for "he seemed to have no proper nose-bridge, so that his nostrils flared out over his cheeks" (p. 15). While the Earl drifts into death the boy goes out to kill an otter in the burn.

From 1065, the date of Thorfinn's death on the Brough of Birsay, the story shifts to 1593 for section three. Using a telling counterpoint, Brown illustrates the iniquity of the reign of Earl Patrick Stewart of Orkney. As we have already seen in 'Witch', Brown makes no secret of his antipathy to the Stewart Earls, Robert (Earl of Orkney from 1581 to 1592) and his son Patrick (who was executed in Edinburgh in 1615). They are remembered for their cruelty and for the architectural monuments they had raised to their vanity. Earl Robert had a palace built in Birsay and, in 'Hawkfall', Earl Patrick sits in his father's palace planning a more splendid palace for himself to be erected in Kirkwall. Though built with forced labour this Earl's Palace in Kirkwall commemorates Earl Patrick's exquisite Renaissance taste. While he entertains a French architect, a man is being tortured in the cellar to make him renounce lands bequeathed to his ancestor William Otter (the boy-servant of Earl Thorfinn). The tormented man, Adam Thorfinnson, has the tell-tale squashed nose. His resistance to torture is futile for Earl Patrick is determined anyway to seize his lands and give him in exchange the poor farm of Lang Klett.

In the fourth section of the story a wedding is brought to the notice of the laird. It is the early nineteenth century. Before their power was broken by the Crofter's Act of 1886 the Orkney lairds pompously lorded it over their tenants by exploiting their land and capacity for hard work. Here the laird cares nothing for his "tenant with the flat ugly nose, Thomas Langclett" (p. 38). What he wants is Langclett's bride and she is summoned so he can exercise his *droit de seigneur*. Thomas Langclett has the stubborn pride of his ancestors but can only impotently stand by and bristle with rage and indignation.

The final section of the story is set in Hamnavoe in 1921.

Humphrey Langclett, general grocer and antiquarian, has forgotten it is the first anniversary of his wife's death. Not so his daughter, a 32-year-old dedicated spinster, who has inserted a memorial note in *The Orcadian*. This is the "death warrant" (p. 50) on the love Langclett feels for a Miss Martha Swift. Unlike his ancestors he is not being tortured by a Stewart Earl or humiliated by an Orkney laird; instead he submissively bows down under the weight of local opinion and pressure from his daughter. He is aware that this means "His generation must perish from the land" (p. 51). The seed that was so vigorous has died out in the gossiping closes of Stromness.

That story has the complexity of a novel compressed into some forty pages. The same literary compression is seen in action in the other major pieces in *Hawkfall*. Before we come to the next major story, however, there is 'The Fires of Christmas', a contrapuntal paraphrase of two incidents from the *Orkneyinga Saga*. At Christmas 1046 Rognvald Brusison and Thorfinn Sigurdson waged a war of fire against each other, with Thorfinn emerging triumphant; at Christmas 1135 Sweyn Asleifson murdered Sweyn Breastrope. According to Brown the fact that Magnus was martyred between these events makes the second the lesser of two evils: "Fate had given way, to some extent at least, to grace" (p. 57). For reasons I make clear in my comments on the novel *Magnus*—the fact that the Orkney saint's death was unavoidable, not heroic—I find this comment unconvincing. However that short piece is succeeded by a fine story, 'Tithonus', in which the eponymous narrator, laird of the island of Torsay, traces the death of his island. The story was suggested by the Greek myth in which Eon (the dawn), in love with the mortal Tithonus, obtains for him Jupiter's gift of immortality but not eternal youth. Consequently, Tithonus is doomed to perpetual decay.

Unlike the laird in 'Hawkfall', this Tithonus is no oppressor. He has no power, no influence, and he has to keep his inherited hall on a legacy of £200 per annum. He has only the title of laird; nothing else remains. Yet his arrival on Torsay is auspicious as it coincides with a totally unexpected birth. An apparently barren couple fifty-one-year-old Maurice Garth and his forty-year-old wife Armingert have been blessed with a daughter Thora. It is the first birth on the island since the arrival of the new laird and he regards it as the dawn of a new era, a sign that the island might renew itself. Too diffident to approach the girl he discovers there is something enigmatic about Thora. His chess-partner, the island schoolteacher, comments on her powerful presence. Tithonus himself confirms this as he watches her stop a pierhead fight with a few words—this at the age of twelve.

Thora leads an unconventional life. She rejects a rich farmer's son in favour of an itinerant and unreliable deck-hand who soon deserts her and her three children. The children are raised to have extreme radical opinions and one of them, a ten-year-old, rebukes the laird, telling him "I'm a communist" (p. 72). The laird's interest in the family is interrupted by illness (double pneumonia). When he recovers he learns that he was expertly nursed by Thora Garth. At the end of the story Thora dies; with her death the heart of the island stops beating (p. 81):

> It is an island dedicated to extinction. . . . Soon now, I know, the place will be finally abandoned to gulls and crows and rabbits. . . . Life in a flourishing island is a kind of fruitful interweaving music of birth and marriage and death: a trio. . . . There is only one dancer in the island now and he carries the hour-glass and the spade and the scythe.

The poignant fact is that in their fifty years on the island together Thora and the laird have never exchanged a word. They have been divided by their stations in life, stations that have ossified into meaningless sterility. Tithonus is a love story with a complete absence of physical love.

A more lively community is presented in 'The Cinquefoil'. This is a portrait in five parts (a cinquefoil is a heraldic bearing representing five frontal petals) of the island community of Selskay. In the first section, 'Unpopular Fisherman' (a title used by Brown for one of the best poems in *Winterfold*), Albert Gurness, a fisherman, tells of a split with his partner Fred Houton because Fred has married Albert's girl, Rosie Wasdale, and turned crofter into the bargain. 'The Minister and the Girl', section two, is made up largely of extracts from the diary of the Rev John Gillespie: wooed on all sides by the women of Selskay, his roving eye falls on Tilly Scabra, daughter of an unruly couple and sister of Albert Gurness's new fishing partner Jerome (all the sections interlock in this way). 'A Friday of Rain' is narrated by "Sailor Jack" Sandside, an old sea-dog so down on his luck he has to beg round the island—this particular Friday in section three he finds that instead of poaching his territory, as he had thought, a kind old woman, Annie, has done his begging for him.

The fourth and most contemplative section—'Seed, Dust, Star'—begins with a discourse on the "permanence and renewal" (p. 105) that sustains an island community, then places this thought in the consciousness of James Wasdale, merchant, who has lost a wife and lost his daughter Rosie: "Age and estrangement and death had removed the seed from his keeping; it was part now of the precarious continuing life of the island" (p. 108). The final section, 'Writings', is subdivided into three parts giving a triple viewpoint of the state of the island. John Gillespie writes to a friend to tell him how his affair with Tilly (now pregnant) has cost him his ministry; a tourist records his impression of a fight between Fred Houton and Bert Gurness; a newspaper account of the same fight reveals that both contestants enjoyed the small explosion of violence. A coda tells us that Bert Gurness has drowned and left everything to his old enemy Fred Houton. Such a promiscuous sequence of events helps form the nature of a community. Brown suggests that a community can survive as long as it is bound together by love (p. 105):

> Most of all the community ensures its continuance by the coming together of man and woman. There will be a new generation to plough and fish, with the same names, the same legends, the same faces (though subtly shifted, and touched with the almost-forgotten, the hardly-realised), the same kirkyard.

Two related stories, 'Sealskin' and 'The Tarn and the Rosary', dwell on the interdependence of art and life, especially art that is rooted in the life of a small community. Orkney folklore is rich in examples of the metamorphosis from seal to human. The legend has been recorded in three ballads: 'The Lady Odivere', 'The Grey Selchie', and 'The Great Silkie of Sule Skerry'.* All three ballads share a quatrain which Brown has modernised:

> I am a man upon the land,
> I am a selkie in the sea,

* These, and other Orkney poems, are collected in ed. Ernest W. Marwick, *An Anthology of Orkney Verse*, Kirkwall (W. R. Mackintosh) 1949.

And when I'm far from any strand
My home it is in Suleskerry.

A selkie is a seal, and Suleskerry is an Orkney skerry. The transformation of selkie into human was used as the basis of one of Eric Linklater's finest stories, 'Sealskin Trousers', in which a man is driven almost insane by the sight of his fiancée joining the seal-folk. Linklater quotes the above quatrain, as does Brown. There the resemblance ends, for Brown is mainly interested in the power of the metamorphic symbol to suggest the "cosmic harmony of god and beast and man and star and plant" (p. 139).

The story begins in the Victorian and ends in the Edwardian period. As it opens Simon Olafson finds a sealskin on the beach; then he finds a naked girl (a selkie who has momentarily discarded the skin). As Simon's mother dies so the family is renewed through Mara, the seal woman. Her son, Magnus, is soon "communing with seals on the rock" (pp. 128–9). In part eight there is an abrupt time-shift and a corresponding change in mood comes after the author tells us "This story is really about a man and his music" (p. 131). Magnus Olafson, son of the seal-woman, is a rich and famous composer. Returning to Norday, his native island, he finds he is treated like an alien. He has lost touch with the place and the folk: he has undergone a metamorphosis from islander to rootless cosmopolitan.

Still, the loss of his primitive folk consciousness has one compensation: he has acquired a first-hand knowledge of the enemy, the new technocrats who want to remake the world in their mechanical image. Simon realises that the function of art is to rediscover the relationship between art and the timeless elements. Thus equipped he can make music that will drown out the sounds of encroaching Progress.

'The Tarn and the Rosary' is complementary to 'Sealskin'. Like 'Sealskin' it is in eight sections, the last of which introduces a shift in time and mood and place. Like 'Sealskin' it is set on the island of Norday. Like 'Sealskin' it has to do with the making of an artist. The interesting difference is that 'The Tarn and the Rosary' deals with the art of literature and the writer, Colm Sinclair, is very much a self-portrait by George Mackay Brown. For, like Brown, Sinclair begins as an Orkney boy naturally gifted at writing; and, like Brown, he

71

becomes a convert to Catholicism. Whereas Brown was bothered by TB, Colm Sinclair has asthma (a switch that is reminiscent of the way Somerset Maugham changed his real-life stammer into a fictional limp in *Of Human Bondage*). Most of all though, the letter that Colm Sinclair writes home could be taken as a succinct synopsis of Brown's artistic and religious beliefs.

The first seven sections of the story deal with Colm Sinclair as an impressionable ten-year-old schoolboy watching life go by: the death of his grandfather; his talks with Jock Skail the tailor (and, as we know from the poem 'The Death of Peter Esson' in *Loaves and Fishes*, Brown had a similar friendship with a tailor); the men in the smithy discussing, with horrific disbelief, the rites of the Roman Catholic church. What means most to the boy is the landscape of Norday, particularly the tarn of Tumilshun. When he reads a Wordsworth poem at school he responds because "It was the interior of Norday that was being bodied forth in a few words" (p. 181). The final section, set in Edinburgh (Marchmont, actually, where Brown had digs as a student at Edinburgh university) describes Colm writing to Jock Skail and defending a novel of his against the charge of Catholic dogmatism. Colm believes in Catholicism because of its beauty and because his own island life convinced him that Christ "came up out of the grave the way a cornstalk soars into wind and sun from a ruined cell" (p. 197). Most of all he has become converted by the insights of religious poets (like George Herbert and Gerard Manley Hopkins).

In Edinburgh Colm feels cut off from his island roots and he decides to go back to Norday, back to the beginning. Before he does he tears up the letter which contains his, and by extension, Brown's statement of belief in the art of religion (p. 197):

> No writer of genius, Dante or Shakespeare or Tolstoy, could have imagined the recorded utterances of Christ. What a lovely lyric that is about the lilies-of-the-field and Solomon's garments. I'm telling you this as a writer of stories: there's no story I know of so perfectly shaped and phrased as The Prodigal Son or The Good Samaritan. There is nothing in literature so terrible and moving as the Passion of Christ— the imagination of man doesn't reach so far—it *must* have been so. The most awesome and marvellous proof for me is

the way he chose to go on nourishing his people after his ascension, in the form of bread. So the brutish life of man is continually possessed, broken, transfigured by the majesty of God.

As an antidote to so much piety and symbolism Brown includes a direct tale like 'The Girl', a realistic portrayal of a group of gossiping crofter-fishermen getting ready for the sea now that the ploughing is over. It is April and they are down in a cove with their boats. On a high sea-bank above the beach a girl lies in the grass waiting for her boyfriend to come on his motorbike. Full of romantic idealism she cannot share the seasonal concerns of the fishermen. The element of romance is explored in a poignant ghost story, 'The Drowned Rose'. This is narrated by Bill Reynolds, teacher in the school on the island of Quoylay. He becomes aware of the presence of his dead predecessor, the beautiful Sandra McKillop, and learns how she found love in the arms of a crofter, John Germiston, while under the influence of the island depression (p. 163):

> There is a trouble in the islands that is called *morbus orcadensis*. It is a darkening of the mind, a progressive flawing and thickening of the clear lens of the spirit. It is said to be induced in sensitive people by the long black overhang of winter.

While out fishing Reynolds discovers that Sandra and Germiston drowned while swimming. Brown uses the ghost-story genre for his own purpose: to show the almost-independent life of strong emotions. Once seized by passion Sandra and Germiston are incapable of rational, commonsensical behaviour.

This Orkney book of the dead closes with a story, 'The Interrogator', whose entire cast are dead. The narrator—the interrogator himself—has come to Norday to investigate the circumstances of the death of a young girl, Vera Paulson, on midsummer day 23 June 1862. Six witnessess are dragged up from the graveyard by Death (with scythe and all); four of them bear false witness. Eventually Vera herself, a "rejected unshriven soul" (p. 213), comes before the interrogator to tell the true story of her death. How, on account of her pregnancy, she was ejected by her father;

almost raped by the ferryman; and rejected by Theodore Helzie, the father of her child. Thus condemned by the spiteful creed of the islanders she gave herself to the sea. This belated confession, it is clear, will ease the agony of Theodore Helzie who has degenerated into poverty and drunkenness. Stories like 'The Interrogator' and 'The Drowned Rose' are remarkable instances of the way Brown can hold the attention of the reader even when the subject-matter seems most unattractive: after all dead heroines are hardly the stuff of romance. The point is that, while death represents a terrible finality for most writers, Brown regards death as a great and provocative mystery. The familiar sight of Maes Howe, that magnificent house of the dead, must have provoked Brown's creative gift often enough. As a result the dead have as much a place as the living in the superbly-constructed house of his prose.

The Sun's Net

If *Hawkfall* is something of an Orkney book of the dead, then the more exhilarating theme of birth dominates in *The Sun's Net* (1976), his most recent book of stories. Four of the ten stories in the book ('A Winter Tale', 'Stone, Salt, and Rose', 'Soldier From the Wars Returning', 'Pastoral') present man and woman in their basic role of, respectively, seed-keeper and seed-nourisher. In *Sweeney Agonistes*, T. S. Eliot described existence as a matter of "Birth, and copulation, and death". Brown holds that religious ceremony imparts a mystical importance to these animal facts of life. His Christianity persuades him that—symbolically at least—all births are to some extent a re-enactment of the birth of Christ. A birth fulfills the promise of the seed; it holds out hope of renewal. In the opening story of *The Sun's Net*, 'A Winter Tale', Brown stresses the religious climate by using the form of a literary triptych (as he had previously done in 'A Treading of Grapes' in *A Time to Keep*). There are three points of view, three separate narratives—that of Dr Clifton, Phil Prinn the schoolteacher, the Rev James Grantham. All three are incomers to the Orkney island of Njalsay and each has a hidden torment which he hopes to conceal on the remoteness of the island. Clifton is a homosexual; Prinn is succumbing to paralysis; Grantham is disturbed by his inability to satisfy either his parishioners or his wife.

The story is set in winter, the season of death. There is a bleakness in the fields though the islanders know there will be a resurrection of their corn—"The corn king dies and rises again and nourishes his people" (p. 22)—to come. Meanwhile Njalsay is "a dying community" (p. 10)—like Rackwick in *Fishermen With Ploughs* or the eponymous village of *Greenvoe*. The young people are drifting away, like snowdrifts, and the doctor foresees a time when the island will be populated only by the dead in the kirkyard. In the week before Christmas there are three deaths: an old man, an old woman and, most deplorable, a young man who hangs himself. The death of the island seems sealed unless a birth can break through its bleak stony exterior.

It occurs to the minister to organise a midwinter feast to which Clifton and Prinn are invited. The evening passes, pleasantly enough, in chatter over drinks and light banter about theology. Priding himself on his contemporary college-trained mind, the minister accepts that biblical miracles might only be myths preserved for the edification of simple people. Clifton's narrative, though, tells how on the way home through the thick snow he is called in to assist in a birth in a deserted croft: "A short time after I entered the hovel a boy was born" (p. 25). In Prinn's narrative we get no reference to this: the strange nativity has completely passed him by. When it is the minister's turn to tell the story he is unable to accept a potentially miraculous event because of his small obsession with trivia. He is worried because the islanders are hostile to his suggestion that they have a model of the Bethlehem crib in the church for Christmas. He does, though, reflect on the strange fact that at Maes Howe each midwinter "a single finger of light seeks through the long corridor that leads into the heart of the chamber and touches the opposite wall with a fugitive splash of gold" (p. 43). So absorbed is he in his private meditation that he is unprepared for a sudden summons to come to a birth in a deserted croft. The nativity also passes him by.

It is a superlative story whose effects are all achieved obliquely. If each birth is an aspect of Christ's birth—a little Story corresponding to the great Christian Fable—the implication is that men have moved so far from ceremony that they are blind to the elemental power that surrounds them. They have come to expect death and to take birth for granted. Although it has its allegorical overtones the sheer believability of the story suggests that this is what it must have been like two thousand years ago in Bethlehem. With hindsight we have plastered the Christian nativity with a thick coat of sentimentality but for contemporaries it merely seemed another birth in squalid circumstances—like the birth in 'A Winter Tale'. Instead of seeing Christ's nativity as a once-in-a-lifetime isolated event Brown's visionary attitude enables him to see it repeated in every birth. In his work miracles happen all the time.

The longest story in *The Sun's Net*—'Stone, Salt, and Rose'—is, at first glance, untypical of Brown. It is not set in Orkney but in Fife; the narrator is not even Scottish but a young English squire, Geoffrey; and, unusually, the story has a completely happy, even fairy-tale, ending which justifies the subtitle 'A Romance'. Yet, as much as 'A Winter Tale', it is simultaneously the Story of a man and a Fable of human seed. It begins, from a Scottish point of view, with a great triumph—the battle of Bannockburn fought (significantly for Brown) on midsummer day 1314. Geoffrey is captured by two Scottish soldiers—a contrasting pair: the kindly Angus and the surly Finn—and brought to Castle Wyvis, home of their master Sir Andrew de Ross.

In Castle Wyvis, Geoffrey is imprisoned in a stone cell (the Stone of the title) and from his window sees, for the first time, the sea (the Salt of the title): "The new element stretched to the horizon, all gléam and serenity and peace" (p. 164). From this window, too, he sees Sir Andrew's daughter, Maud (the Rose of the title), emerging naked from the North Sea. Intruding on his love for the sea and his longing for Maud is the reminder that Geoffrey is a prisoner and, as such, compelled to write a ransom note to his father though he knows his family will find it hard to raise the stipulated one hundred English crowns. When the money fails to materialise Geoffrey is made a serf and set to work in the oatfield. It is as if a vindictive Fate had held out its hand to crush him. His future appears to be nonexistent.

Unknown to Geoffrey, he is actually being put to the first of a series of tests that will determine whether or not he is fit to sow his seed in Scotland. His appetite for manual work proves his physical strength. To test his virility a local girl Morag seduces him, on the orders of Sir Andrew, and he passes this with flying colours for Morag is soon carrying a fine son. His third and final test is to go on a dangerous voyage to the massive castle of the infamous Latvian robber-baron Schvein. Although Schvein is secluded in mourning for his homosexual lover Vladimir, Geoffrey's manner is so impressive that he is presented with a peacock for Sir Andrew. By now he has demonstrated his strength, his virility, his courage. On his return to Scotland, Geoffrey is taken before a company including his own father, Sir Andrew de Ross and King Robert the Bruce himself. They are there to see Geoffrey, "the seed-keeper" (p. 217), married to Maud.

In his previous three books Brown had presented stories that were mainly variations on a theme so that the symbols were occasionally more substantial than the human beings (for example, the title-story of *A Calendar of Love*). In 'Stone, Salt, and Rose' he is interested in the operation of the narrative itself so we have a more conventional, sequential style without counterpoint or abrupt time-shifts. This method is more suited to the unadorned style Brown sometimes uses in *The Sun's Net*. 'Stone, Salt, and Rose' is followed by another tale that takes the battlefield as the point of departure for a voyage. 'Soldier From the Wars Returning' is a tale in which an elemental urge overcomes defeat and death. In 1650, with Cromwell triumphant and Charles executed, James Graham Marquis of Montrose returned from exile in Holland to make his last royalist stand. He recruited more than a thousand Orkneymen, an untrained force easily defeated by David Leslie's dragoons at the battle of Carbisdale, near Bonar Bridge. The narrator of Brown's story has been shot dead in the battle; unable to accept his death he becomes a homing ghost heading for his farm seven miles from Hamnavoe so he can be reunited with his girl Marion, his Penelope. Slowly, during the odyssey back to his sources, the fact of his death dawns on the ghostly narrator. He is now, he realises, irrelevant to the needs of the earth because he is incapable of renewing life. He can no longer pass on the seed. As for Marion she has her natural place in the preservation of life: "For a country girl like Marion love is simply the hunger in her womb for the seed" (p. 229). Accepting this insight the ghost is content to die completely.

Like 'Stone, Salt, and Rose', 'Soldier From the Wars Returning' is an attempt to make the reader believe that impossible events possibly happened. Both stories are austere, with a relative absence of imagery and ornament. Both are like transcriptions of dreams (and it is worth remembering that Edwin Muir found much of his poetic material in dreams). The fourth seed-story, 'Pastoral', has a realistic texture and is tragic in tone. It is an account of a man who sowed one wild seed too many. Master Blyth, the narrator, is a factor troubled by the outbreak of sheep-stealing in his parish (so the text consists of his letters to the absentee laird). The local men bring him James Tormiston, a crofter-fisherman, and pronounce him guilty of sheep-stealing. Now he is clearly innocent of that charge but blatantly guilty of impregnating as many of the local lassies as he could lay hands on. When the factor discovers that his daughter too has been impregnated he turns the young crofter-fisherman over to the authorities in Kirkwall to be hanged. This grim account of revenge has an ironical ending for the future of the parish will depend on the results of Tormiston's fertility.

The remaining six stories in *The Sun's Net* offer more thematic diversity than is usual in Brown's closely unified collections. Two of them are in the minor key, 'Silver' and 'The Seven Poets'. 'Silver' is an anecdote about a fisherman going on an unsuccessful odyssey to find his Penelope (Anna Taing) who has, in the meantime, disappeared to marry a student. It is given shape and depth by the way Brown teases out the implications of the word "silver": the silver coins the landlord is paid with; the silver chain the fisherman hopes to retrieve; the silver shine on the three haddocks he carries. 'The Seven Poets' is an allegory dedicated to the memory of the Scottish poet Sydney Goodsir Smith who died in Edinburgh in 1975. In the aftermath of a nuclear holocaust the earth has renounced technology and created village communities: the narrator visits poets in Spain, Mexico, Sweden, Africa, Siberia, Iceland and "thirty years later, I find myself for the first time among the mountains of Scotland" (p. 268).

The holocaust theme is frequent in Brown's writing: in *Greenvoe*, in *Fishermen With Ploughs*, in stories like 'The Seven Poets'. It is an extension of Brown's conviction that Progress is likely to come to grief in a mindless abuse of technology. Machines are always treated as soul-destroying eyesores: the anonymity of great urban conurbations is contrasted, in 'The Seven Poets', with Brown's ideal—"small villages of not more than 250 people" (p. 257). It might be objected that this is a naive notion, that the world would remain in the dark ages were it not for the material benefits of Progress, that Brown's work seeks to avoid the problems created by the industrial revolution. Yet Brown does not state his case in terms of strident argument; he seeks to persuade the reader by the healing power of his images. Just as Yeats had his gyres or Graves his White Moon Goddess, so Brown has his own myths that offer an artistically valid alternative to the positivist claims of modern science.

But back to Orkney: 'The Book of Black Arts' is a fine example of Brown's skill at reworking stories from Orkney folklore. As a child Brown heard the story of this book—a jet black volume with a diabolical Latin text printed in white letters. It was supposedly circulated at a terrible cost to those who were tempted to use its powers. The book had to be purchased so that each owner could use it to make terrible mischief: afterwards it had to be sold at less than cost-price until it came to one who paid a farthing. Such an unfortunate would go to hell. In Brown's story the Book is sold to a Hamnavoe landlord for "one flagon of whisky, value a shilling" (p. 55)—a price that sets the story in the distant past. After using it to bewilder his patrons and give his tavern a lucrative infamy the landlord loses everything in a thunderbolt. He sells the book for sixpence to Rob Skelding, a poor farmer envious of the fertile farmland of his neighbour.

Rob uses the Book to get "one marvellous year of fertility" (p. 68) from his land—and a corresponding barrenness in the land of his neighbour—before his fields are blighted again and death comes to his crops and himself. Swart the blacksmith buys the Book next, for a penny, and is changed from a benevolent man to a braggart whose one aim is to destroy the only man who has defeated him at wrestling. He does so, but at a terrible physical cost, and sells the book for a farthing to the sexually frustrated district nurse Teenie Twill. She uses it to get a man but the ensuing child dies while Teenie herself is ostracised in the parish until she takes the Book to the minister who burns it. Throughout, this tale is enlivened by Brown's vivid pictorial imagination as, for example, when Rob Skelding rewards his men (p. 66):

> Rob gave his helpers a half-sovereign each to take home with them; like splinters of the fruitful sun the coins lay in those dark country hands.

That image is more telling when we remember how important coins are to the sense of the story.

Even when the content of a story assumes supernatural proportions, Brown's method is to weave into his imaginative variations enough ordinary indigenous details to make it convincing. Such is the case with 'The Book of Black Arts' and also the story that follows it, 'Brig-O-Dread'. The inspiration comes from the old anoymous poem 'A Lyke-Wake Dirge', particularly this quatrain:

> From Brig o' Dread when thou mayst pass,
> — *Every nighte and alle*,
> To Purgatory fire thou com'st at last;
> — *And Christe receive thy saule*.

In his collection, *The Labyrinth* (1949), Edwin Muir leaned on the theme for his dreamlike 'The Bridge of Dread' in which there is a "flower of fire". The notion of a fiery Purgatory is central to Brown's story. He, however, invokes the Orkney setting and the Brig-O-Dread becomes the Bridge of Brodgar which divides the Loch of Harray from the Loch of Stenness, "the twin lochs with the prehistoric stone circle" (p. 100). Brown establishes the mood so well—a mixture of realism and fantasy—that poetic speculation is given the weighty assurance of folk wisdom (pp. 102–3):

> Time is a slow banked smoulder to the living. To the dead it is an august merciless ordering of flames.

Protagonist of the story is Arkold Andersvik, a fifty-year-old Hamnavoe man who serves on the town council and runs a shop selling whalebone mementoes—carved by his brother Wistan—to tourists. This brother, lazy and inclined to drink too much, shoots Arkold then makes it look like suicide. Arkold prepares for the afterlife by writing a conceited account of his life in which he portrays himself as a model citizen, an exemplary husband, a fine father. He has to pass into Purgatory where the flames of truth will scorch this account. As a ghost, Arkold begins to see himself as others see him: he is unlamented, criticised by his widow, cursed by his brother. Still, the flames of truth prepare him for heaven and he is to be judged by a jury of his favourite cultural figures, Chopin, Jane Austen, Van Gogh.

It should come as no surprise, with this writer, that the road to heaven is a stroll through a pleasant, heavenly, ideal village community (p. 114):

> The villagers ... began to gather round the table. ... Mugs and pieces of bread were passed round — there was a mingling of courtesy and banter.

To object, on sociological grounds, that such an image of perfection is hopelessly limited is to miss the point. Brown is compelled, by his artistic integrity, to give a recognisable shape to his poetic dreams and for him the good small community — lacking the puritanical negativity he often rebukes in small Orkney communities — is something solid enough to believe in and to make believable.

Finally, there are two interdependent stories, 'Perilous Seas' and 'The Pirate's Ghost', both concerned with the eighteenth-century pirate John Gow. From his window in Mayburn Court, Stromness, Brown can see the spot where Gow's pirate ship anchored in 1725. No doubt this brought the story into being for Gow is surely Stromness's most infamous son. He was born in Caithness and raised in Stromness where his father was a respectable merchant. Because he was an "honest open lad, well-educated too" (p. 119) Captain Oliver Ferneau of the ship *Caroline* made him his second mate. On 5 November 1724, while the *Caroline* was sailing from Santa Cruz to Genoa, Gow — who had been entrusted with the ship's firearms — led a mutiny and murdered Captain Ferneau. He then renamed the ship the *Revenge* and embarked on a career of piracy.

This story of local-boy-makes-bad was sufficiently attractive to fascinate two celebrated authors before Brown got to grips with it. Daniel Defoe wrote an account (the sole surviving copy of which is in the British Museum) of Gow's trial and execution. Sir Walter Scott used Gow as the model for Captain Cleveland in his novel *The Pirate*. In 'Perilous Seas' Brown contents himself with putting some flesh on the bones of the story of the mutiny so that the principal characters — Gow, Captain Ferneau, first-mate Jelfs — assume fictional lives and move in an atmosphere of menace. It is in the second story, 'The Pirate's Ghost', that Brown comes into his own.

'The Pirate's Ghost' takes place at the beginning of 1725. Gow has come home to Stromness as the seemingly illustrious captain of the *George* (the third name given to the *Caroline*). He is a welcome guest at the home of James Gordon, a Stromness merchant, who encourages the twenty-five-year-old Gow to make discreet advances to his daughter Thora. However, the outrageous behaviour of Gow's crew makes the locals suspicious and eventually the terrible truth about Gow is revealed by his pursuers. Before he flees from Stromness Gow makes a love-pact with Thora at the Stone of Odin, five miles from the town: "John Gow and Thora Gordon had only one night for the mingling of their fires" (p. 152).

Gow is captured, taken to London, tried and hanged (twice, for the first attempt is botched) at Execution Dock, and his body is tarred and left hanging for the perusal of the public. The pull of love is too strong for Gow's ghost and it returns to Stromness to haunt Thora, constantly crying for release from her love. Gow's ghost must be one of the most revolting in literature, all decay and filth and torment. To release it Thora goes to Wapping and shakes hands with the tarred corpse. Personally, I prefer Brown's more symbolic stories but adventure-yarns like the two pieces on Gow show how well Brown can command a simple brisk narrative pace when he wants to.

Tales for Children

The four collections we have considered contain sixty stories and Brown has told me he has some thirty more in hand, so further collections will follow in the course of time. As well as these mature stories he has published two books of tales for children: *The Two Fiddlers* (1974) and *Pictures in the Cave* (1977). These show him at his most economical, deploying a direct uncomplicated narrative. They retell folk tales in a delightfully original way. The title story of *The Two Fiddlers*, for example, is based on the same legend of Storm Kolson's stay in the Trowieknowe used by Brown in *A Spell for Green Corn*. The other stories manage to preserve the best of Orkney folklore: events like James V's incognito adventures ('The King in Rags'); the battle of Summerdale ('The Battle in the Hills'); 'The Everlasting Battle' between the petrified armies of two kings. The Orkney ballad 'The Lady Odivere' becomes a charming story, 'The Seal King'; and the legend of 'The Vanishing Islands' of Eynhallow and Hether-Blether is made very matter-of-factual. Brown—who has fond memories of his own island childhood—never writes down to children but tries to engage their imaginations by demonstrating that the world of fantasy is valuable, not a mere distraction. Only in his introduction to *The Two Fiddlers* does he allow himself a proselytising note (p. 10):

> Now, alas, the story-making gift is waning in the islands; and will wane increasingly as we watch our television serials on a winter evening, and read sordid ugly 'real' stories out of the newspapers.

It should be obvious by now that Brown's own work refutes this allegation, that in fact the story-making gift is alive and well and living in Stromness.

4   Dramatist and Novelist

So far we have examined Brown's mastery of short forms like the poem (the sequence *Fishermen With Ploughs* remains a series of interdependent poems) and the story. He has, however, written three extended pieces: the play *A Spell for Green Corn* (1970); and two novels, *Greenvoe* (1972) and *Magnus* (1973). In these his abiding interest in form and shape has served him well so that the situations become that much richer, and the voyages that much more involved. The gift for symphonic construction is seen at full stretch. Apart from the consideration of length the stylistic features are as recognisable as before: the indigenous landscape of Orkney, the pressure of history on the present, the mingling of Story and Fable, the evocation of the miraculous, the use of folklore.

Plays

A Spell for Green Corn is Brown's only published full-length play, though 'Witch' (*A Calendar of Love*) is written in dramatic form and the closing scenes of *Magnus* originally appeared as a dramatic dialogue between the tinkers Jock and Mary in *An Orkney Tapestry*. At the end of *An Orkney Tapestry*, too, there is a short play in two scenes "suggested by Tolstoy's marvellous story, 'What Men Live By'; otherwise they are as different as a skerry from a steppe" (p. 4). This play, 'The Watcher', presents a miracle in Hamnavoe. Samuel Innertoon, a poor cobbler, rescues from the winter cold a naked man, Michael. He speaks hardly at all but his "smile is like a kindling of sticks in a cold empty place" (p. 196) and his eyes see angels and visions. He rewards Samuel's kindness by instantly mastering cobbling and helping him to increase his reputation and wealth. He also sees the angel of death hovering round the overweening Orkney laird who owns Hamnavoe. After this exposition there is a short sharp climax; a fishing boat has been presumed lost at sea but the crew turn up at Samuel's door to thank Michael for saving them (p. 211):

> Michael pulled us out of the sea, one after the other. Then he led us up the face of the Craig, to the top. We're beholden to him.

Yet Samuel's wife swears that Michael never set foot outside the house. Michael is an angel and in Brown's work it is not too unusual for angels to walk naked in the street of Hamnavoe. Brown's prose enchants us into believing that miracles can, and do, happen all the time.

Apart from 'The Watcher', Brown has completed a play, *The Holy Voyage*, about Earl Rognvald's crusade; has written a radio play about the history of Rackwick, *Gray Furrow, Black Furrow*; and is working on a play about the Irish monk Brendan who, according to one tradition, discovered America in the eighth century. All this suggests that Brown is becoming increasingly interested in the possibilities of plays combining conversational naturalism with the fabulous framework. It will be fascinating to watch his progress as a dramatist. He has also provided the libretto of an opera, *The Martyrdom of St Magnus*, for the composer Peter Maxwell Davies who has a house in Rackwick and who has set Brown's lyric 'From Stone to Thorn' (*Winterfold*) to music.

A Spell for Green Corn

A Spell for Green Corn was first performed on the BBC Third Programme in October 1967 but, as printed, reads as a stage play. It brings together several elements that have caught Brown's creative attention. There is the folklore about the Trows, the tiny fairy-folk supposed to dwell in the neolithic burial mounds. One legend, recounted by Brown in *An Orkney Tapestry* (p. 128) and used as a children's story in the title-piece of *The Two Fiddlers*, tells of the disappearance of a fiddler one midsummer eve:

> The fiddler had been stolen by the earth people; not by the winter trows, who are all famine and deformity, but by the good trows, the potent energies of the earth that quicken

grass and corn. They had stolen the fiddle so that its music would make the corn tall and golden under the sun that summer.

This fiddler, Storm Kolson, is the principal character in *A Spell for Green Corn*; his presence activates a strong response in others, and his absence (when he is taken by the trows) is used as an excuse for a communal act of insanity.

Into the fabric of the play Brown also works his belief in a miraculous past when the simple (Catholic, of course) faith of the people produced miracles out of commonplace objects; and his conviction that the Knoxian Reformation destroyed this miraculous relationship between the earth and the folk in the name of Progress. And walking through the centuries spanned in the play are the timeless tinkers Isaac and Sarah, eternal witnesses to all things. Brown also uses the dramatic idiom to contrast the hesitant speech-rhythms of a young girl with the harsh certainty of a puritanical factor; and to juxtapose both types of speech with the artistic splendour of two original ballads.

The play opens on "The island of Hellya, Orkney, in the age of saints and fish and miracles" (p. 9). The islanders are lamenting the loss of their finest fisherman, Erik, and are reluctant to take the advice of a monk—Brother Cormac—that they should turn from fishing to crofting, that they should cultivate a sea of corn instead of risking their lives in the real sea. To convince the island folk, the monk performs a miracle by transforming a stone into a fish, a symbolic enactment of the agricultural metamorphosis of earth into food. The tinker is the first to eat the fish and the folk have a new faith. The first scene, 'Miracle', ends with the magnificent 'Ballad of John Barleycorn' in which a furrow asks a ploughman the fate of the corn; and the ploughman shows her how it has been changed into bread and whisky (pp. 14–15):

> I took a bannock from my bag.
> Lord, how her empty mouth did yawn!
> Says I, 'Your starving days are done,
> For here's your lost John Barleycorn.'
>
> I took a bottle from my pouch,
> I poured out whisky in a horn.

Says I, 'Put by your grief, for here
Is the merry blood of Barleycorn.'

She ate, she drank, she laughed, she danced.
And home with me she did return.
By candle light in my old straw bed
She wept no more for Barleycorn.

That ballad can stand comparison with the traditional ballad, 'Sir John Barleycorn', on which it is based—and with the version by Robert Burns.

The second scene, 'Witch and Poet', switches the chronology to 1663. It is midsummer eve, the time when Orkney folk light a great Johnsmas fire on the summit of the highest hill believing that the man-made conflagration would reflect the midsummer sun and that the whole celebration of light would guarantee fertility. However the Reformation has come to stay and the power to reckon with on the island is John Rosey, the absentee laird's factor. He stands for all the repressive, naysaying, kirkified, anti-papist doctrines that Brown dislikes. He is a personification of Progress. He calls Storm Kolson's fiddle "a potent instrument of the devil" (p. 18) and the midsummer fire "a relic of papistry and superstition" (p. 19). After upbraiding Storm Kolson for his licentious behaviour and taking his fiddle from him, Rosey arranges a marriage between his own daughter Thora and Kolson who is, after all, the son of a merchant and therefore a good catch. When he is approached by Sigrid Tomson, a blameless young woman concerned about the general indifference to the midsummer fire, Rosey gives her Kolson's fiddle to burn.

Without his fiddle, a symbol of folk art, Kolson is full of foreboding. He meets a foreign sailor whose six shipmates have drowned because their ship has been deliberately lured onto the rocks of Hellya by a light. Kolson drinks with the sailor but is convinced that, without music, the island is doomed. When he meets Sigrid at the site of the midsummer fire she tells him "The corn's dead" and he replies that "The word is lost" (p. 28). The folk, having succumbed to the negativity of the Reformation spirit, are without faith and art. Kolson's immediate answer is to make love to Sigrid while she, for her contribution to vitality, rescues Kolson's fiddle from the fire. Because of his magical music—putting a spell on the green corn—the islanders remember the ancient midsummer rituals. The corn will be saved.

A short third scene, 'The Tinker Road', establishes that Kolson has disappeared after playing at the Blinkbonny wedding; however "The whole island's tossing with gold" (p. 34). The scene is a dialogue between Isaac and Sarah and into Sarah's poor mouth Brown places a second superb ballad (pp. 33-4):

> There stood three men at the black furrow
> And one was clad in yellow.
> They're led the fiddler through a door
> Where never a bird could follow.
>
> They've put the gowd cup in his hand,
> Elfin bread on his tongue.
> There he bade a hunder years,
> Him and his lawless song.

The fourth scene, 'The Wrong Word', has Rosey accuse Sigrid of being a witch, mainly on the grounds that his daughter has been deprived of a provider since the disappearance of Kolson. The blatant evidence of Sigrid's innocence—like the innocence of Marian Isbister in 'Witch' (*A Calendar of Love*)—is beside the point. Once the wheel of vengeance is in motion it can only gather momentum. So in the fifth scene, 'A Red Coat for Sigrid', we are taken to the Market Cross before Saint Magnus Cathedral in Kirkwall for a ritual burning ("a red coat" is Brown's customary kenning for death by burning). Brown describes the full horror of Sigrid's fate by emphasising the insensitivity of the crowd. Their gossip betrays the fact that the burning is, for them, a distraction. Among the crowd Sigrid glimpses Storm Kolson.

The final scene, 'Resurrection', is set in the twentieth century, "The age of machines and numbers and official forms" (p. 54). It is the day of the Hellya Agricultural Fair whose bizarre attractions are as crowd-pulling as the seventeenth-century witch-burning. The tinkers Isaac and Sarah reappear as Ikey and Sal in the Social Security tent. They are after money. Though time has passed the elemental situation remains constant for, after the tinkers, we are reintroduced to Freya who featured in the first scene as the woman of the drowning sailor, Erik. Then Storm Kolson reappears as the Blind Fiddler. The Social Security clerk can make little of them: Ikey and Sal are malingerers; Freya is still searching for her lover; Kolson gives his age as three-hundred-and-twenty-five when he applies for his fiddle to be restrung.

Normal notions of chronology collapse as Brown brings together all the previous features in the play, so that the finale is like a musical recapitulation. The Blind Fiddler is not only Kolson but the drowning sailor from the first scene; Freya becomes Sigrid. Kolson makes an eloquent speech, shot through with archaisms, about the sacred bond between art and the rhythm of life (p. 62):

> Maskers, know that in God's gift lieth a mystery like unto holiness, a shadow of creation, a far sweet whisper. This is it, art—what ye call poem, pattern, dance. One cold act of beauty (in default of sanctity) might yet flush the hill with ripeness.

As a loudspeaker off stage announces a Pageant of Machines, the Blind Fiddler, Storm Kolson, realises he has one more task, to confront Progress with the power of art: "There's one thing you and I must do yet, fiddle, we must break the machines" (p. 66).

In an appendix to the play Brown offers what are purported to be seventeenth-century records relating to a witch-trial. These are totally convincing documents, impeccably written in the manner of seventeenth-century prose, yet they are all the original work of Brown. His expertise at duplicating the stylistic idiom of the past is uncanny and he demonstrates this linguistic virtuosity often enough for it to be a strong feature of his total artistic outlook. In a document entitled 'Storm Kolson's Notebook', Brown expresses his belief that the finest art becomes the public property of the folk (p. 89):

> Printing was nearly the worst invention of all. Once men cut their music and poems on stone, mere hints and suggestions. The imagination of the listener was compelled to the service the art.

It is Kolson's (and Brown's) belief that art must have a function, a magical purpose, if it is to deserve a permanent place of value among the people. If art is merely decorative it becomes one more distraction—like an agricultural side-show, or the burning of a witch. Instead (p. 83):

> Art must be of *use*—a coercive rhyme, to strand a whale on the rock, a scratch on stone to make the corn grow. What are all these fiddles and statues and books for?

In Brown's case the books are for preserving the heritage of the past. He wishes to bring its richness to bear on the spiritual poverty of the modern world. What happens when a community exists without art or compassion or love is that it is easily disposed of. It becomes no match for modern technology. The consequences of this are to be seen in Brown's first novel.

Greenvoe

Greenvoe was published in May 1972 when George Mackay Brown was fifty, a late start for a first novel. The author was not, of course, a novice but a man with five collections of poetry and two collections of stories behind him. Moreover he was a man who had already mapped out the artistic territory he was interested in exploring. What was novel about *Greenvoe* was the way in which Brown showed how magnificently he could sustain his thematic material over such an extended structure. For *Greenvoe* is not a conventional novel in the sense of the steady unfolding of a gripping narrative—in fact all the really dramatic action is compressed into the last chapter. It is rather the imaginative investigation of a way of life as it is revealed through various people who together make up a community. The village of Greenvoe (meaning green-bay) on the imaginary island of Hellya (the same island cited in *A Spell for Green Corn*) is well on the way to self-destruction; outside events simply make the death more dramatic.

Ostensibly the novel describes the five typical days that precede the official demise of Greenvoe. The year is 1968 and Greenvoe survives on fishing, farming, and gossip. The men of Greenvoe gravitate to Bill Scorrodale's Greenvoe Hotel while the women congregate around the village shop run by the scheming Joseph Evie and his bitter wife Olive. The whole set-up looks like the parochial fag-end of an insular existence where, as one of the locals puts it (p.

19), "Here we are much as usual. Not a thing happens in this place." Always a writer who sees several sides of a situation, Brown presents the story of the fall of Greenvoe on three distinct levels.

The first level is the immediate present and the technique employed is fictional realism. What happens on this everyday level revolves around three fishermen: Bert Kerston whose habitual drunkenness corresponds to his wife's endless nagging; Samuel Whaness, an industrious fisherman who awaits the coming Knoxian heaven in the company of his barren wife Rachel; and The Skarf, a devout Marxist, who has forsaken fishing to write up the history of the island. During the days that follow Bert Kerston gets beaten up by his son for neglecting his pregnant wife; Samuel Whaness almost drowns when he gets out of his depth, both literally and theologically; and The Skarf imposes his history of Hellya, an "arrogant slanted rigmarole" (p. 110), on anyone who will listen. These three men are clearly differentiated but they all have the fisherman's love-hate relationship with the sea that sustains them and torments them; gives them a livelihood and threatens their lives.

Still on the level of fictional realism, Brown contrasts the lives of this trinity of fishermen with the lesser characters in the book. Ivan Westray, ferryman and modern Viking, makes erotic overtures—urgently in the case of Miss Margaret Inverary, the sexually frustrated schoolteacher; contemptuously in the case of Inga Fortin-Bell, the laird's grand-daughter. Alice Voar, twenty-nine-year-old spinster, has seven children by different parents and her uninhibited sensuality is counterpointed against the near-mindless cogitations of Timmy Folster, a meth-drinking beachcomber. Timmy is not the only one who drinks, however; we learn that the parish minister Simon McKee is an alcoholic with quite a few skeletons in his drink-cupboard. His mother, old Mrs McKee, is haunted by the ghosts of her presbyterian conscience. Calvinism has taught her to be plagued by guilt, so she is sure she must be to blame for the moral weakness of her son.

Such is the state of affairs in Greenvoe, but the island has a rich Orkney history and the historical narrative—the second level of significance—is presented through The Skarf. What he writes in "an old cash-book that Joseph Evie the merchant had thrown out" (p. 10) comprises the heritage of the island. In four stretches of historical narrative The Skarf tells the story of Hellya. After the first shadowy settlers had come to the caves of Keelyfa, an adventurous Mediterreanean people had come with their sacred jar of seedcorn and their architectural ability to build the Broch of Ingarth at Keelyfa so they could keep out invaders. The Viking invaders, though, swept all before them and one of them, Thorvald Harvest-Happy, brought agricultural expertise to the island. In this way the great circle of life could flourish: the sun could bring corn out of the earth. After the Vikings came feudalism, then capitalism, and The Skarf awaits the coming of the Marxist Millennium. His ears are constantly attuned for the coming "music of the Children of the Sun" (p. 259).

The Skarf's dream is not central to the book: his presentation of the past is. For his words show how the Broch of Ingarth is the seminal point of the island. Near this Broch, in the year in which the novel takes place, a timeless ritual is being observed at the Bu farm. This is the third level of significance, ritual symbolism; and it is enacted in dramatic form. We are introduced to the members of the Ancient Mystery of the Horsemen, a secret society who meet in the stable of the Bu, three miles from Greenvoe. According to the rites of this society old Mansie Anderson of the Bu is Lord of the Harvest. During the novel he takes his son Hector through the six initiation rites of the Ancient Mystery of the Horsemen. The six rites embody, in symbolic form the crucifixion and resurrection of corn. A stone symbolises death; the lifting of the stone allows life to break through again just as corn shoots through a field cleared of stones or as Christ rose again when the stone was removed.

Greenvoe is divided into six chapters and—given the importance Brown attaches to numbers—there is nothing arbitrary about this. The six chapters correspond to the six stations in the initiation rites of the Ancient Mystery of the Horsemen. Each chapter ends with a station and a dusk so that the next chapter can open with the dawn of a new day full of the possibility of renewal. Chapter One contains the Station of the Plough; chapter Two the Station of the Seed; chapter Three the Station of the Green Corn; chapter Four the Station of the Yellow Corn; and chapter Five the Station of the Dead. It is at this point—the opening of the sixth and final chapter—that the measured pace of the novel changes abruptly so that instead of another day a catastrophe dawns on Greenvoe, the technological catastrophe embodied in Operation Black Star.

For into the everyday life of Greenvoe has come a mysterious guest to stay at Bill Scorrodale's hotel. He is isolated in his room, deliberately cut off from the people. He sits alone all day and rumours buzz like bees around his person. Some of the locals surmise that he might be a writer but Ivan Westray asks rhetorically (p. 158): "How the hell can a man write a book about a place if all he does is sit on his arse at a typewriter?" Eventually the guest is seen for what he is through the eyes of an Indian packman Johnny Singh (who narrates chapter Three in the form of a letter to his uncle). The man is yet another personification of Progress (p. 99):

> He is a bureaucrat. He is Western Man arrived at a foreseen inevitable end. I see it now. He rules the world with a card index file.

He has come on behalf of Operation Black Star, a military-technological project that requires the island of Hellya—but not its people. So the village is to be flattened, the community aborted, the past obliterated. The mechanical present is to be imposed on the island regardless of the needs or wishes of the people.

Inevitably Operation Black Star brings wealth to some—to the Evies, to Bill Scorrodale, to Ivan Westray. Timmy Folster it brings to an institute in Kirkwall, while old Mrs McKee fades away into a second childhood. Bert Kerston gets a job as a ghillie on Hrossey (the Norse word, meaning "island of horses", for the Orkney mainland); the Whanesses go to Hrossey to stay with Rachel's brother; Miss Inverary goes back to Edinburgh. The Skarf is briefly employed as a clerk with Operation Black Star then, when it is discovered he is a Marxist, he is sacked. He gives himself to the sea, drowning in a dream of the Song of the Children of the Sun. Most dramatic of all, though, is the recalcitrance of Mansie Anderson of the Bu, the symbolic Lord of the Harvest. He is politely indifferent when he is told the authorities want to sink a gateway to Black Star through the cornfield of the Bu. His resistance is short and bitter; he is forcibly evicted from his land. After all this destruction the authorities abandon Operation Black Star fifteen months after its inception. They leave and they seal off the island so that it cannot be contaminated by humanity.

Ten years later on midsummer eve Mansie Anderson returns with seven men to Greenvoe. Like the men who brought the sacred jar of seed-corn to Hellya they land at the cliffs of Keelyfa; then they make for the Broch of Ingarth (p. 277):

> Round here they had sown Hellya's first grain and reaped its first harvests; this was where they had made their music and laws and myths. This navel had attached many generations of Hellyamen to the nourishing earth.

They had come to complete the last station in the initiation rites, to invoke the spirit of resurrection. By this symbolic act they hope to restore agricultural life to the island; in its wake this will bring back people. So the future of Hellya depends on their response to the midsummer sun. The book ends as the seven men stand in the sun suffused with the promise of resurrection (p. 279):

> The Lord of the Harvest raised his hands. 'We have brought light and blessing to the kingdom of winter', he said, 'however long it endures, that kingdom, a night or a season or a thousand ages. The word has been found. Now we will eat and drink together and be glad'.
>
> The sun rose. The stones were warm. They broke the bread.

Brown's use of the dimension of timelessness—a device that allows events to endure the passing of chronological time—brings before the reader a world where renewal is always a possibility. Given faith and the richness of the earth life will survive. In Muir's great poem 'The Horses' the world survives a nuclear holocaust when it is reborn in an Orkney agricultural community. In *Greenvoe* the world is reborn through the utterance of the Word of God, resurrection. At the end of the Rackwick chapter in *An Orkney Tapestry* Brown explicitly stated his belief in the possibility of renewal and rebirth through the cultivation of the earth (p. 51):

> I do not think Rackwick will remain empty for ever. It could happen that the atom-and-planet horror at the heart of our

civilisation will scatter people again to the quiet beautiful fertile places of the world.

At first glance it seems hopelessly innocent to believe that technology can be overcome by a determination to return to a rural life enriched by myth. But Brown is not advocating a political programme; he is offering a gift of imagery. The visionary nature of his work can at least stimulate people to consider their roots and to question whether in promiscuously embracing a mechanical god of Progress something valuable and elemental might be lost. Something that civilisation can ill afford to lose.

Technically *Greenvoe* is a *tour de force*, a bravura stretch of prose that is made memorably poetic by the sheer force of the images. If we think of an image as a verbal picture projected onto the imagination so as to make the mind focus sharply on an otherwise unfamiliar object—then we shall realise how powerful Brown's images are. We will realise too that the images are completely integrated into the novel. Rachel Whaness, the barren wife of Samuel, desires children so much that there is something poignant about her gift of haddocks to Alice Voar, so gifted with fertility that she has the obligatory seven children (p. 27):

> 'Very kind of you, Rachel', said Alice Voar, and held the bunch of three up by the string. The glancing underwater quicksilver was leaving them; they were touched with the tarnish of death; soon they would be grey stiff headless gutted shapes on a big blue plate.

Again, the sustaining sea is brought to bear on the body of Inga Fortin-Bell; she emerges from the water like a mermaid as she waits to test the passion of the modern Viking, Ivan Westray (p. 126):

> Her hair was plastered in black strands about her throat and shoulders, and her body was pearled with salt-drops.

Pearled with salt-drops: the metaphorical precision of the language projects a vivid picture of sensuality.

Rather than present a continuous narrative, Brown has divided his text into episodic fragments that have a contrapuntal interdependence. Several things happen simultaneously. We are aware of the past (Skarf's narratives) and the timeless symbols (the drama of the Mystery of the Ancient Order of Horsemen). The montage has to be rearranged in the mind of the reader. The Tolstoyan method of the multiple viewpoint enables Brown to present a solitary event as if it were seen through the various facets of a prism. For example, it is incidental to Inga Fortin-Bell's erotic daydream (p. 125) that, lying and thinking of D. H. Lawrence's story 'Sun', she is startled by the "chug-chug of a motor-boat"; that she then "squinnied at the name on the bow, shading her eyes: *Siloam*". However, pages later, while the reader is still in some suspense as to what will happen in the coming confrontation between Inga and Ivan Westray, we get the viewpoint of the presbyterian Samuel Whaness on the *Siloam* (pp. 129–30): "That shameless hussy was still lying on the table-rock. Samuel Whaness turned his eyes away sternly. She was even more naked than before". This expert manipulation of the multiple viewpoint gives depth and conviction to the writing.

The only time the episodic technique is suspended is when Mrs McKee's imaginary prosecutor presents to the court the evidence of the old woman's responsibility for Simon's alcoholism. This lasts for twenty-six pages (pp. 183–209) and really constitutes a marvellous short story in itself, the tale of a hypersensitive man seeking spiritual solace in drink. Throughout that sequence, throughout the book, the texture of the prose is appropriately rich. Like Dylan Thomas in *Under Milk Wood*, Brown delights in the familiar poetry offered by a catalogue of everyday objects (p. 122):

> Mrs McKee gathered the cups and plates, the marmalade pot, Simon's quarter-eaten egg, the toast-rack, the butter-dish, the cream-jug, the sugar-bowl, the salt-and-pepper, the teapot, the crusts, on to a tray, and carried it through to the kitchen.

A mundane, yet lively, list of that sort brings the prose down to earth so that the provocative symbols relate to a real world. At the end of the book, as the village of Greenvoe collapses around her, the old infirm Mrs McKee is used as a vehicle to convey, symbolically, the image of time collapsing, going into reverse back to the birth and beginning of her wayward alcoholic son (p. 255):

> she was young again. . . . She remembered . . . Simon awash . with lupins and dew; Simon's head in lamplight, bent over his theology books; Simon constellated with measles . . . Simon quiet as apples in his cradle; the slow throb and curve and quest of the foetus in her womb.

Whoever the narrator, the dominant sound through the book is the supple, suggestive, persuasive voice of George Mackay Brown. When The Skarf presents his narrative he does so in the style of Brown. When Johnny Singh writes home to his uncle he does so in the stylistic idiom of Brown. When the prosecutor torments Mrs McKee with the evidence against her he does so in the euphonic metaphor-studded prose of Brown. Direct speech is another matter. The speech of the villagers is elegant and cadenced, a true facsimile of Orkney speech for, as Brown says in *Greenvoe* (p. 15), the islanders' "speech was slow and wondering, like water lapping among the stones". This is best seen in the many scenes in the village shop when the various women—Rachel Whaness, Alice Voar, Ellen Kerston— think aloud and independently, wrapped up in their own worlds.

In one instance, though, Brown radically alters the nature and texture of his prose, and this is to convey the mood of a man near to death. As that man is the puritanical Samuel Whaness the style is biblical. We have already seen—in stories like 'Witch' (*A Calendar of Love*)—that Brown has a great command of archaic idioms. The whole sequence of Whaness's flirtation with death resuscitates the prose of the bible. It is approached by Brown's characteristic methods. First, there is the use of the multiple viewpoint. Throughout chapter five, Hellya is surrounded by a terrible fog (more real than symbolic) but Samuel Whaness, going perilously close to the Red Head crags in pursuit of lobster creels, sees through it (pp. 175–6):

> For one fleeting second that morning the veil of the temple was torn, and through the dazzling rent Samuel saw the Skerries lighthouse three miles away, and the sun hurrying across the shredded tissue of fog.

After that, just as he is mesmerised by a clump of seapinks, his boat is engulfed by waves and he accepts that God has come for him (p. 177):

> The grey dome collapsed utterly. Samuel was resting instead under a dome of crystal, of purest light. Joy flooded all his veins ... he set out, smiling, to discover the habitations of the saints.

Samuel imagines he is being watched by God. Using the multiple viewpoint, though, Brown makes it clear that it is not God's eye that is on him but the indifferent eye of Inga Fortin-Bell who is at that moment standing inside the lighthouse (p. 180):

> Once [the fog] split completely open, and she could see for a moment the western cliffs of Hellya in diffused sunlight, and a little fishing boat under the Red Head.

From Inga's viewpoint—emotionally affected by Ivan Westray—the plight of the boat is a small thing, a waterdrop in the scale of the ocean. Samuel is hopelessly at sea, out of his depth.

It is at this point that Brown inserts into the perilous saga of Samuel Whaness the long passage about Simon McKee's alcoholism. When we encounter Samuel again the prose is completely biblical and he is on his way, hopefully, to heaven (p. 214):

> Now were the feet of Samuel grown heavy and stained with travel, for after that first pure access of joy in the temple the keeper of the gate thereof revealed to him by fair words that he was by no means come yet to the City of God. ... And he put a staff and a lanthorn into Samuel's hand for to help him on his journey, and fastened stout sandals upon his feet.

In his brush with death Samuel passes the people of Greenvoe and imagines finally that he sees a drowning Bert Kerston in his boat and bends to give him the kiss of life. Just as he had reversed time to convey Mrs McKee's second childhood; so Brown brings us back to reality with a memorable image of the kissing men changing places so that it is Kerston saving Samuel and not vice versa as the biblical prose suggested (p. 223):

> The kiss transformed everything: for the body seemed to mingle with his, to rise up and through him, to stand high above him; and his own body fell through the drowning with an amazed cry. He was a slobbered face laid obliquely on the bottom of the boat.

That sort of dynamic image makes the prose vigorous and startling.

There is a literature of rural decay behind *Greenvoe*: Goldsmith's 'Deserted Village' and the work of D. H. Lawrence—who is mentioned in *Greenvoe* by Inga who has read *Women in Love* and the story 'Sun'—are obvious examples. Brown does not simply echo this literature—which deifies the organic society at the expense of industrial civilisation—for he does not blame the destruction of the village of Greenvoe entirely on Operation Black Star (p. 244):

> Greenvoe shrivelled slowly in the radiance of Black Star. It was obvious, of course—even the Welfare Officer admitted that—that the village was moribund in any case, a place given over almost wholly to the elderly, the fatuous, the physically inept. Black Star merely accelerated the process.

Brown has said, in *An Orkney Tapestry* (p. 76) that "In a wholesome society the different estates are stitched together in a single garment"; in Greenvoe the land was neglected, the fishermen divided (Kerston and Whaness argue constantly over lobster creels). Brown sees the fundamental problem as a matter of preserving the ancient elemental rhythms that motivate an ideal community. These rhythms can be supplied by folk art or, more dramatically, by the waves of passion that follow martyrdom.

Magnus

Without art and, in Brown's book, without religion any community will wither. The idea of redeeming society by weaving the Seamless Garment pervades his second novel *Magnus* (1973). The image is a biblical one (*John* 19:22):

> Then the soldiers, when they had crucified Jesus, took his
> garments ... and also his coat: now the coat was without
> seam, woven from the top throughout.

This Seamless Garment of Christianity can be rewoven by a saint, we are asked to believe. And who better than the Orkney saint, Magnus, who had long fascinated Brown. In the text for a tourist guide, *Let's See the Orkney Islands* (1948), the stream of information is interrupted at one point by Brown's definite opinion that "Near Rousay lies a little island, Egilsay, on which, in 1116 AD, occurred the most vital event in all Orkney's rich history—the martyrdom of Earl Magnus" (p. 56). In his first book of poems, *The Storm*, Magnus appears twice—in 'The Road Home' and 'Saint Magnus on Egilsay'; and in his first collection of stories, *A Calendar of Love*, the significance of Magnus is mentioned in two stories, 'The Three Islands' and 'Stone Poems'. A key chapter in *An Orkney Tapestry* deals with the martyrdom of Magnus and there are frequent references in Brown's work to the magnificent St Magnus Cathedral in Kirkwall which was founded by Earl Rognvald in 1137 as a monument to his saintly uncle.

Some twenty years after Magnus's brutal death his life was recorded, in Latin, by an Orcadian priest Master Robert; the events of Magnus's life are also contained in the *Orkneyinga Saga*. These accounts, and the scholarly biography of *St Magnus—Earl of Orkney* (1935) by the Kirkwall businessman John Mooney, are the sources of Brown's novel. He has, naturally, translated the recorded events into his own artistic terms. Basically, though, the story is briefly retold. When Earl Thorfinn, Orkney's mightiest ruler, died, his earldom passed into the joint care of his sons Paul and Erlend. This divided rule was inherited by Paul's son Hakon and Erlend's son Magnus. For seven years the two contended for sole control of the islands before agreeing to a peace conference on Egilsay at Easter 1117 (the exact date varies between 1115 and 1117). As the cousins had agreed, Magnus arrived with two ships; Hakon, on the other hand, came with eight. When the landowners of Orkney insisted on an immediate solution, the politic Hakon put himself forward as the most suitable ruler. Magnus, realising the danger he was in, tried to save his life by suggesting that he be banished or imprisoned. The Orkney landowners would have none of this: death was to be the final solution. Magnus then accepted the inevitability of death: he was executed by Hakon's cook Lilolf who, at Magnus's request, hammered the axe into his forehead. In 1919 the shattered skull of Magnus was found in a secret tomb in St Magnus Cathedral. The story is immensely dramatic but it is difficult for a non-Catholic to see what was particularly saintly in Magnus's murder: he tried to avoid death then humbly accepted it. What else could he do?

Having succeeded in creating a completely believable community in *Greenvoe*, Brown accepted the challenge of recreating the life of a recognised saint in *Magnus*. Fiction is not usually an ecclesiastical medium but *Magnus* often reads like a theological discourse with fictional asides. If, as I have suggested, the man Magnus had no choice in the matter of his death (his only contribution being a request to dignify the manner of his going) then Brown would have had a difficult task in making the martyrdom completely convincing. As a Catholic, though, he tacitly assumes that the martyrdom was ordained by God and in the novel we have to take Brown's faith for granted.

In *An Orkney Tapestry* (p. 87) Brown says "The story of Magnus and Hakon unfolds like a drama. Some day a play will be written about it; I have not the ability myself". He must have felt, however, that he had the ability to write a novel about it, if not a play. With his mastery of prose and access to a wide repertoire of effects—from the archaic idiom to a parody of modern popular journalism—Brown surely felt he could scan the saga account of Magnus's life and isolate the quality of saintliness. In order to do this he would have to rely on an other-worldly atmosphere; and he would have to depend, as never before, on the symbol. In *Magnus* he claims (p. 140) that "The symbol becomes a jewel enduring and flaming throughout history. . . . Men handle the jewel and know themselves enriched."

Still, the opening of Magnus directs the reader to the very earthiest level of existence. Mans, the peasant representative of common humanity in the novel, has to plough Revay hill facing the tidal island, the Brough of Birsay. His ox is lame so Hild, his woman, has to pull the wooden plough so they can make seven furrows on the hill. Counterpointed against this are events that Mans can only see at a distance on the Brough of Birsay. A wedding is taking place between Erlend and Thora. The title of this first chapter, 'The Plough', underlines the symbolic nature of impregnation. The peasants thrust their seed into the furrowed earth; Erlend sows his human seed in Thora, the mother of Magnus. As the peasants finish their work Erlend and Thora embrace in bed and the seed of Magnus is planted (p. 26):

> a great sacrificial host surged between the loins of bridegroom and bride, and among them a particular chosen seed, a summoned one, the sole ultimate destined survivor of all that joyous holocaust.

In this astonishingly intimate way Magnus is deliberately set apart from the other characters in the novel. He is "chosen", he is "summoned". He has been put on earth for a divine purpose. His other-worldliness is contrasted with the earthiness of Mans who speaks with the voice of the oppressed through the ages. There is no attempt to portray Mans as simply a man of his time, a twelfth-century peasant. Mans is timeless, he is downtrodden man, and his indignant complaint against the world could well issue from the voice of a modern radical (p. 20):

> The honest labourers, they're kept under by a few parasites. Yes, parasites.... A parasite is a person who does no work, no, but he lives in luxury all the same. And who provides the parasite with his silks, and his silver and his flagons? *I* do.

Anachronism is, in fact, one of the main stylistic features of *Magnus*. Magnus and Mans: twin aspects of mankind, the saint and the sower of seed. In his reluctant way Mans works his own agricultural miracles by lifting stones so that the corn can rise in an image of resurrection; Magnus is not to be so lucky. Although a radical, Mans is glad there are folk for him to look down on, the tinkers John and Mary who stroll through poverty and miracle and time in *Magnus*. The likes of Magnus, the ruling classes, are held in contempt by Mans.

Magnus is not, nor was intended to be, principally a novel of action. Its essence is meditative rather than dynamic. To put the still, timeless, discursive parts of the book in perspective, however, Brown makes sure that the action, when it occurs, seethes with incident. After a brief account of Magnus's monastic education in chapter two, 'A Boy and a Seal', we are plunged in the third chapter, 'Song of Battle', into violent action. This is the battle of the Menai Straits, 1098, fought between Hugh the Proud, earl of Shrewsbury; and King Magnus of Norway. Simulating the alliterative style of heroic poetry, Brown conveys the brutality of the battle (p. 57):

> Then a second arrow struck the Earl of Shrewsbury on the face: it shattered nose-plate and nose and passed on into his skull. The body was borne backwards by the impact.

As an antidote to this hyperbolic manner there is Mans, peasant pressed into military service, who is there because he has been ordered to become an oarsman. When he thinks everything is going the King of Norway's way he tries to get into the thick of things for a bit of vicarious glory (p. 59):

> He gave a wild yell and leapt into the Welsh ship with his axe raised. He slipped in a pool of blood. He fell on his backside among a strewment of corpses.

Between these conventional extremes of heroic king and comical peasant there is the still centre of the personality of Magnus. In the *Orkneyinga Saga* there is an account of Magnus's unexpected behaviour:

> While the men were unsheathing their weapons and making ready for fight, Magnus Erlend's son sat down aft in the well, and made no move to arm himself. The king asked why he was sitting down. He said he had no quarrel with any man there;—"therefore I will not fight".
> [Then] said the King: "Go down under the deck, and lie not here among men's feet, if thou durst not fight; for I do not think that religious belief is at the bottom of this".
> Magnus took a Psalter and sang through the fighting but did not go into shelter.*

In Brown's novel this incident becomes the first real example of Magnus's singularity: "Magnus Erlendson was still unrolling the

---

* A. B. Taylor, *The Orkneyinga Saga*, Edinburgh (Oliver and Boyd) 1938, p. 199.

psalter in the bow as if it was Evensong in the Birsay church" (p. 55).
Among the splendidly described clatter and din of battle Magnus
retreats into religious introspection; while all the others are being
swept along on a rushing torrent of descriptive prose Magnus acts
with a quiet dignity. He is not like other men; he is not, in other
words, willing to kill on a king's command.

Clearly Magnus is no ordinary Viking warrior, and it is at this
point—in the third chapter entitled 'The Temptations'—that we
begin to understand why. He is being guided by an angel called The
Keeper of the Loom who tells Magnus he is to take the loom of the
spirit and weave upon it an immaculate garment—the Seamless
Garment of sanctity. In this way Brown deprives Magnus of a free
will: his actions are predetermined by an angelic adviser. This is
hard to swallow for the non-Catholic reader, especially as the angel is
a conventional biblical one—unlike the angel in the poem 'The
Stranger' (*Loaves and Fishes*) or in the short play 'The Watcher' (*An
Orkney Tapestry*).

From this point on, the novel becomes a meditation on Christ's
parable of the marriage feast (*Matthew* 22) which, as Brown reminds
us, is "that parable in which Christ compares the celestial kingdom
to a marriage feast, and how it is good for a guest to wear to the feast
his wedding garment lest, having some inferior garment on, he is
shamed and put out into the darkness" (p. 137). Magnus's entire life
becomes a quest for this suitable wedding garment, this Seamless
Garment of sanctity. Brown is quite explicit on the symbolism of the
garments. There are, in fact, not one but three. The first is the "coat
of diurnal hand-to-mouth existence" (*An Orkney Tapestry*, p. 77)
whose everyday social protection embraces all levels of society
(though some are a great deal more equal than others). This
everyday coat is described by Mans who tells Prem the weaver (p.
96):

> ... we're all one folk. We all hang together, we're all of a
> piece. Priest, ploughman, laird, tinker, earl, we're all woven
> together in a kind of coat.

With the onset of war between Magnus and Hakon, Mans adds, "the
coat's in tatters and Orkney's naked".

The second coat is the coat-of-state and this is entirely heraldic. It is worn by the Earl of Orkney in assembly and for putting official seals on decrees. When worn by the Earl "In a mystical way it gives warmth and dignity not to the chosen wearer alone, it enwraps the whole community" (p. 111). In the novel the predicament is that two men—Hakon and Magnus—both lay claim to this heraldic, ceremonial coat-of-state, thus threatening to destroy the whole fabric of society by bringing it into disrepute. The hand-to-mouth coat is a practical covering; the coat-of-state represents a concept that embraces the people and gives them the sense of belonging to a unified society. It is an ideal to cling to; without it society is hopelessly weakened.

The third coat is the Seamless Garment of sanctity, the white coat of innocence, the immaculate garment. To wear it is to become Christ-like and sacrificial. The spectacle of a man assuming this sacrificial role binds a people together with an awareness of the highest aspirations of man. The sacrifice implies salvation for the whole community. It is this coat that Magnus must wear at the marriage feast. Before he can assume this Seamless Garment, however, he must gain control of his own soul by facing five temptations. First, he uses the psalter instead of the axe at the battle of Menai Straits; thus resisting the temptation of killing designated enemies. Second, when consumed by lust, he cools himself with holy water. Third, he resists consummating his marriage to Ingerth so he will remain a virgin. Fourth, he refuses a tempting offer to become sole Earl of Orkney because it means that Hakon must be murdered. Fifth, he turns down the chance to become a monk at Eynhallow because he knows he must not quietly withdraw from the world but be martyred so the world will know of his sacrifice. There must be a valid reason for this sacrifice.

We find this reason in the appalling condition of the coat-of-state. Because of the civil war in Orkney the islands are being destroyed. This is symbolised by the scarecrow that gives its name to chapter five. The rule of law has collapsed and the ordinary people—like Mans and Hild—are terrorised by the capricious brutality of the horsemen who roam the countryside murdering at will and trampling over the life-sustaining cornfields. Again it is Mans, the rebellious Everyman, who rebukes the horsemen for destroying the corn (p. 96):

'You're trampling on the bread of the people!' yelled Mans from the edge of his field.

In the light of the halo that is soon to descend on the broken head of Magnus it is worth noting that both sides are equally brutal. Their political coloration—black patches for Magnus, red patches for Hakon—does not affect their inhumanity.

After an interlude of a chapter, 'Prelude to the Invocation of the Dove' (in which Bishop William of Orkney cogitates on the coat-of-state/Seamless Garment dilemma and receives a delegation determined to settle the divided Earldom) Brown comes to the climax of the novel—chapter seven, 'The Killing'. With his gift for brisk vigorous prose it would have been feasible to convey this death in the dynamic style used to describe the battle of the Menai Straits. However Brown does not so much want to involve the reader cathartically in the drama of the killing as make him reflect on the matter, make him consider it analytically as an event of timeless significance. In order to do this Brown has recourse to various Brechtian *Verfremdungseffekte*—unexpected techniques of distancing the reader from the cathartic flow of fictional narrative.

Magnus himself appears at the opening of 'The Killing' as a dreamer: he is wrapt in contemplation of the parable of the marriage feast, wondering how he can attain a suitably holy garment. He ignores a clear natural warning—a freak wave that signals danger—and sails on to his fate on Egilsay. At this point Brown anachronistically shifts the action of the novel to our own time by seeing the arrival of Magnus and Hakon through the eyes of a modern popular journalist. Thus he implies that the martyrdom is as relevant today as it was in the twelfth century. Brown piles on the anachronistic details—there are binoculars and photographs and telephones and guns—so that the reader feels very much in the journalistic present. Having established this dramatic time-shift Brown switches the mood again; this time he presents an erudite essay on the symbolism of the Roman Catholic Mass. Here there is a danger—no more than that—of Brown sacrificing his own creative gift on the altar of Catholic dogma because the excess of theological doctrine vitiates the otherwise sonorous prose.

The first part of the exposition of the symbolism of the Mass has the fifty-four-year-old Magnus watching an old priest and a young boy participating in the Catholic ceremony. Magnus is aware of the presence of his guardian angel, The Keeper of the Loom, and realises that the Mass presents a vivid image of eternity (p. 139): "All time was gathered up into that ritual half-hour, the entire history of mankind". His mouth has been searching for a word and at last he finds it: *Sanctus*. He accepts his fate, accepts the fact that he will not leave the island alive. He decides to spend the night in the church. While he is closeted with the painful knowledge of his imminent death and subsequent sanctity the means whereby this will be achieved occur inexorably. The Orkney landowners force Hakon to choose between his own death and that of his cousin Magnus. Being only human Hakon suggests that Magnus should be the one to die. When his standard-bearer refuses to carry out the execution Hakon appoints his cook Lilolf as a suitable man for the job. In this Brown follows the details given in the *Orkneyinga Saga*. The action is suspended again as Brown returns to the discursive method for a consideration of the question of ritual sacrifice.

According to Brown primitive people, such as those who worshipped round the Ring of Brodgar, required a bestial sacrifice: they spilled the blood of an ox on stone. In more fanatical societies human sacrifice was the order of the day. Civilisation advanced by abolishing the human sacrifice and substituting a ritual sacrifice so that images were offered in the place of flesh and blood. However, there came a moment when civilisation was so sick that God himself had to come down to earth and sacrifice himself. This is Brown's interpretation of the foundation of Christianity. This supreme sacrifice renewed the meaning of the images used in ritual sacrifice: Christ's body became bread and his blood wine. Roman Catholic ceremony was established as a permanent ritual of sacrifice. To a humanist like myself it is possible to see the crucifixion of Christ as a socially-sanctioned mass murder of one vulnerable individual whose message of equality was unsettling to the guardians of the state. Brown, however, takes the view that Christ was actually divine so that, instead of suffering real agony, he "endured gladly the fourteen stations of his death-going" (p. 169). Although the saga account of Magnus's death deprived him of any volitional decision—for Hakon and the landowners had already decided he must be killed—Brown suggests that Magnus walked willingly to his death (p. 170):

> So Magnus Erlendson, when he came up from the shore that
> Easter Monday, towards noon, to the stone in the centre of
> the island, saw against the sun eleven men and a boy and a
> man with an axe in his hand who was weeping.

Determined to press home to the reader the contemporary
relevance of his theme, Brown has recourse to another of the
Brechtian *Verfremdungseffekte*. He transfers Lilolf to the twentieth
century and makes him a cook attendant on a concentration camp.
This modern Lilolf takes up the story in his own words. Lilolf's
confession makes it absolutely clear that for Brown the particular
sacrifice is The Sacrifice, a timeless event that is perpetually
reenacted. For the man Lilolf executes is not Magnus but Dietrich
Bonhoeffer, the Lutheran pastor who was hanged by the Nazis at
Flossenburg on 8 April 1945. The parallel here is weak, I feel,
because Magnus—on the evidence of the novel and its source, the
Orkneyinga Saga—passively accepted his execution. There was
nothing he could do about it, and it came after he had indulged
enthusiastically in civil war. All he contributed to the event was the
detail that he should be struck on the forehead—and not
beheaded—in a manner appropriate to his aristocratic rank.
Bonhoeffer, on the other hand, was an active opponent of the Nazi
regime. He became involved in the resistance to Hitler and was
prepared to pay for his activism with his life. Brown's acceptance of
the Catholic version of sanctity tends towards credulity.

In Lilolf's narrative two vagrants appear; they are the tinkers Jock
and Mary come to witness the deeds of the twentieth century. In a
very earthy way they connect the twentieth to the twelfth century.
They are the eternal watchers over misfortune and human cruelty.
Appropriately, then, the last chapter of Magnus—'Harvest'—is
given over to them. (This chapter is in fact an expansion of the
dramatic conclusion to the Magnus chapter in *An Orkney Tapestry*.)
Mary is now blind and Jock takes her to Birsay kirk (where Magnus's
body was taken) so he can pray to Magnus to restore her sight. One
of the difficult things to accept in the novel has been the shadowy
figure of the principal character, Magnus, and here Brown tries to
describe his spirit (p. 204):

> This man was now in two places at once. He was lying with
> a terrible wound in his face in the kirk near where the old

man and the old woman were girding themselves for the
road: Birsay, place of his beginning and end, birth and
sepulchre. Also he was pure essence in another intensity, a
hoarder of the treasures of charity and prayer, a guardian.

This fragrant vivid ghost was everywhere and always, but
especially he haunted the island of his childhood.

Magnus responds to Jock's prayer and Mary's sight is restored. With
the voice of the monks of Birsay in his ears Jock thanks the future
saint (p. 206):

> —*Saint Magnus the Martyr, pray for us.* . . . . Jock the tinker said it
> before any of you.
> He put the empty sack over his shoulder and turned and
> moved off after the sea-washed feet of Mary.

Magnus is, technically, an immensely ambitious novel. The
counterpoint between Mans and Magnus, the use of Brechtian
Verfremdungseffekte, the exhilarating mixture of heroic and contemplative prose, the frequent time-shifts: these testify to a rare
literary gift. Where the novel does suffer is when the author
succumbs to the danger of reification—the taking of symbols for
material objects. The whole novel hangs on the image of the
Seamless Garment of sanctity. If we remain unmoved by this image
we must inevitably find flaws in the novel. An image illuminates a
text but cannot entirely comprise it. In *Greenvoe* the symbolic
material was successfully integrated with reality because we were
impressed by the brilliantly close observation of a whole community
of characters. In *Magnus* only the peasant Mans and the tinkers Jock
and Mary are given a solid fictional identity. Magnus is conspicuous
by his corporeal absence. No doubt this was the intention of the
author but he owes it to non-Catholic readers to explore the man
Magnus instead of dogmatically accepting his sanctity.

The danger of reification is acknowledged at one point
when Magnus's five fellow-pupils from Birsay—who never emerge as
more than names—are agreed that (p. 117) "One and all they
disliked the tropes and figures and images that churchmen use."

Although my own admiration for *Magnus* is qualified by a
reluctance to accept wholeheartedly its dogmatic elements (for I

cannot see anything particularly saintly in a man being murdered—and that is what happens in the novel for a non-Catholic reader) it must be said that the book contains some of Brown's most sheerly beautiful writing. The resurrection-of-the-seed image is fully stated in all its impressive symbolism (pp. 93–4):

> Now that the seed was uttered upon the land the peasants waited for the sun and the rain to do their bit. What they had performed was an act of faith. They trusted that the seed they had buried would return from the grave, first the shoot, then the ear, then the stalk with a full burden of corn in the ear. But this yearly resurrection of the seed was encompassed with dangers. The rain might fall in black deluges on the hill all the month of June. The sun might shrivel the crop with unwonted ardency while it was still green. More terrible still, the black worm might bore into the root.

Here, though, we are on familiar symbolic territory. At the end of the book there is a corresponding image of the life-giving sun (p. 202): "The sun rose—the harvest sun—an immense vat of thick red primeval clay, brimming with corn and ale for all the bewintered people of the world."

It may be that Brown had lived so long with his faith in Magnus the saint that the writing of the book was done more in the nature of a religious duty than a stimulating act of creation. For the moment he has no plans for further novels because, he says, "I don't particularly like the novel form". I think it is something he will return to, though. Each novel took a year to write—the time it takes the earth to go round the sun, an annual odyssey. Brown likes to compare his work with that of crofters and fishermen and for them, too, there is a completion, a perfection, in work that unfolds during a year, through the four seasons. The symbolism of that might well prove to be an overwhelming temptation for George Mackay Brown.

5   A Timeless Voyage

It is a respectable literary practice, when examining the work of a contemporary writer, to award him a measure of restrained praise followed swiftly by some stern strictures. I have abandoned the practice in this monograph because I am convinced that Brown is not only a major modern literary figure but a man who has so completely mapped out his own artistic territory that he competes with no one: his work and life are suffused with a spirit of generosity. To disagree with certain of Brown's beliefs—his Roman Catholicism, for example—would be to treat his work as the arid expression of a rational argument. Yet he is not a prophet or a preacher; he is a superb artist offering a unique vision. Those who do not see eye to eye with the vision need not be blind to the quality of the images. In his great poem 'Hamnavoe' Brown describes a day in the life of Stromness then says, with reference to his father,

> In the fire of images
> Gladly I put my hand
> To save that day for him.

What his work does is to save a rich island past for the modern reader. It is a gift for which we must be grateful.

Certainly there are features in Brown's work that might irritate some. He is isolationist in outlook and an obdurate enemy of Progress. This one-man resistance to the modern world—whose technological and medical miracles Brown might well set against the religious miracles he believes so fervently in—can result in sourness. It is pointless to complain as bitterly as he does that modern life has left folklore behind. He says in *An Orkney Tapestry* (p. 21):

> The old stories have vanished with the horses and the tinkers; instead of the yarn at the pier-head or the pub, you are

increasingly troubled with bores who insist on telling you what they think about Viet Nam or the bank rate or heart-transplants, and you may be sure it isn't their own thought-out opinion at all, but some discussion they have heard on TV the night before, or read in the *Daily Express*—and now, having chewed it over, they must regurgitate it for you.

No, modern man is not as pathetic as that; his scientific analysis of the world is not a betrayal of the past. And in cultivating an awareness about the rest of the world he is expressing a common humanity. In his *Letters from Hamnavoe* (p. 41) Brown considers the environmental dangers inherent in the discovery of oil round the Orkney coast: "we can bid a swift farewell to the Orkney we know. ... That Orkney is about to vanish as drastically as Pictish Orkney once the Vikings arrived. Much that is precious and irreplaceable will be no more". As an opinion, that undermines Brown's use of depopulation as a dreadful omen (with young people going to the cities and leaving the islands to the dead in the kirkyards). The prosperity provided by oil might well reverse the tendency to depopulation and surely Orkney can absorb people from Industrial Scotland with grace. If the Ice Age, the Stone Age, the Bronze Age and the Viking era can provide Brown with so much artistic material, why not the Age of Oil?

Sometimes the logic of Brown's work suggests that the only salvation for the world is in the creation of a primitive agricultural community in the wake of a terrible nuclear holocaust. This, of course, is what Muir imagined in his poem 'The Horses'. The problem, though, is not to obliterate civilisation—to utter a vindictive death-wish on Progress—but to humanise technology with the imaginative power of art. After all, man cannot live by symbolic bread alone and even George Mackay Brown has reaped some of the benefits of Progress. He may be a reluctant benefactor but he has still genuflected at the shrine of technology. For example he can say, in *Letters from Hamnavoe*, first that (p. 11) "Portable transistors are one of the very worst inventions of our time", and later admit (p. 26) "when the other week I received a small windfall—a literary prize from France—with part of it I bought a transistor set".

It is also apparent that some of Brown's works are constructed to fit a mathematically precise formula consisting of the number seven, a voyage, a jar of seed-corn, and nubile women ready, willing and able to receive human seed. This formula, it has to be said, has never let him down but I was delighted when he wrote to me to say "I've been trying some poems and prose poems in (for me) a new mode: don't know what I'll think of them in six months' time". So there may yet emerge a new shade of Brown. We will have to wait and see.

These, though, are small criticisms that do not alter my admiration for Brown's work: to disagree with him is one thing, to deny the awesome power of his work would be sheer folly. Brown's work is beautifully shaped for survival. It is like a vast ocean over which shine starlike images and symbols. He takes us on a timeless voyage on the ocean and makes us aware of the profound depths beneath the glittering surface.

Bibliography

1 Poetry

The Storm, Kirkwall (The Orkney Press) 1954.

Loaves and Fishes, London (The Hogarth Press) 1959.

The Year of the Whale, London (Chatto and Windus/The Hogarth Press) 1965.

Twelve Poems, Belfast (Queen's University Festival Publications) 1968.

Lifeboat and other Poems, Bow, Crediton (Richard Gilbertson) 1971. Limited edition of 100 copies.

Fishermen With Ploughs, London (The Hogarth Press) 1971.

Poems New and Selected, London (The Hogarth Press) 1971; New York (Harcourt Brace Jovanovich) 1973. Contains thirteen new poems and selections from *Loaves and Fishes* and *The Year of the Whale*.

Selected Poems, London (The Hogarth Press) 1977. An expanded—by eleven poems from *Fishermen with Ploughs*—edition of *Poems New and Selected*.

Penguin Modern Poets 21, Harmondsworth (Penguin Books) 1972. Contains selections from *The Storm, Loaves and Fishes, The Year of the Whale, A Spell for Green Corn, Fishermen with Ploughs, Poems New and Selected*, as well as selected poems by Norman MacCaig and Iain Crichton Smith.

Winterfold, London (Chatto and Windus/The Hogarth Press) 1976.

2 Stories

A Calendar of Love, London (The Hogarth Press) 1967; New York (Harcourt Brace Jovanovich) 1968.

A Time to Keep, London (The Hogarth Press) 1969; New York (Harcourt Brace Jovanovich) 1970.

Hawkfall, London (The Hogarth Press) 1974.
The Two Fiddlers, London (Chatto and Windus) 1974. For children.
The Sun's Net, London (The Hogarth Press) 1976.
Pictures in the Cave, London (Chatto and Windus) 1977. For children.
Witch and other Stories, London (Longman Heritage of Literature Series) 1977. With commentary and notes by D. M. Budge.

3 Novels

Greenvoe, London (The Hogarth Press) 1972; New York (Harcourt Brace Jovanovich) 1973; Harmondsworth (Penguin Books) 1976; London (Longman Heritage of Literature Series) 1977, with commentary and notes by D. M. Budge.
Magnus, London (The Hogarth Press) 1973; London (Quartet Books) 1977.

4 Drama

A Spell for Green Corn, London (The Hogarth Press) 1970.

5 Others

Let's See the Orkney Islands, Fort William (W. S. Thomson) 1948. Text for illustrated tourist guide.
Stromness Official Guide, London (E. J. Burrow) 1956. Text for illustrated tourist guide.
An Orkney Tapestry, London (Victor Gollancz) 1969; London (Quartet Books) 1973. Essays on Orkney.
Letters from Hamnavoe, Edinburgh (Gordon Wright) 1975. Selected journalism from *The Orcadian*.
Edwin Muir, West Linton (Castlelaw Press) 1975. A memoir.

A recording, George Mackay Brown, *in which the poet reads twenty-four poems and an extract from the story 'Witch', was issued by Claddagh Records, Dublin (CCA 6) in 1977.*

Index